IN HER SHOES

UNLEASH THE SPARKLE OF SURVIVAL

PRESENTED BY: YVONNE GEORGE

Your story is not over yet.

This book is dedicated to every woman who has had to overcome some of life's greatest challenges. It's my heart's desire that these stories will encourage and inspire other women that "they too" can get through what they are going through. No one should ever feel alone or ashamed because of what they have had to endure.

I was born with a spirit of compassion, and have felt the burden of others suffering as if it were my own from an early age. Watching others struggle made me realize how important it was to be there for one another. However, that took on a whole new meaning when I experienced my own pain and felt alone and ashamed. It wasn't until others shared what they had been through that my own healing began. I realized at that point how valuable it was to have someone hold you by the hand and utter the words.... "I understand what you are going through." Their own pain was used to heal mine.

You never really can understand what a woman goes through unless you have been "In Her Shoes." You learn that your pain is an opportunity to learn a lot about yourself. You learn that what you go through "GROWS" you. You learn that no matter what, people will accept you and love you even though you have been broken. Some of these stories have never been told before now. I applaud each one of these authors for coming forward and speaking out about their pain and suffering in hopes that it may help encourage and inspire someone else heal from their own adversity they may be facing. For these twelve brave women, I can honestly say they know how to UNLEASH THE SPARKLE FROM WITHIN!

Yvonne George
Founder/ Principal owner
YvonneGeorge.com
Live Your Sparkle

There is a light in this world, a healing spirit more powerful than any darkness we may encounter. We sometimes lose sight of this force when there is suffering, too much pain. Then suddenly, the spirit will emerge through the lives of ordinary people who hear a call and answer in extraordinary ways.

~Mother Theresa~

In Her Shoes:
Unleash the Sparkle of Survival
Our Stories

Rebecca Bergman.. 6

Kimmberly Ramos... 20

Monika Guzman.. 32

Regan Adams-Snyder...................................... 45

Stephanie Owen Albert.................................... 52

Allison Byrd-Haley... 65

Debbie Hemingway.. 69

Corrie Wells... 77

Yolanda Contreras Taylor................................. 91

Amanda Cooper... 111

Tina LaRea.. 122

Lisa Corrales.. 135

REBECCA BERGMAN

What one word would you use to describe yourself and why did you choose that word?

One word that I would use to describe myself would be passionate! The definition of passion is a strong feeling of enthusiasm or excitement for something or about doing something. I chose each day to live my life with a passionate heart!

This word best describes me because, I am passionate about sharing God's love with others, I am passionate about loving my family and being a good wife. I am passionate about raising children to live their life with purpose. I am passionate about women finding their strength and being empowered by life's challenges and love themselves just as they are. I live a passion driven life. I was once told being passionate doesn't define you. I disagree with that statement. I believe that being passionate does define me! I passionately believe that when you seek to be passionate about what you are doing and how you are doing it, that passion defines your level of heart and drive to succeed in all things! I do all things with great enthusiasm and love for others. I seek to not just live my life for me but to live as a testament to others. I know I am doing good things for others and living to be the woman I know God created me to be!

Share with us about an experience you faced that challenged you and placed you in a situation where you had to make tough decisions? How did you overcome it?

My life much like a lot of people became challenging at different stages. When I was a young girl I dealt with not feeling like I was good enough. I was the second child in a family of six. My mother had a lot on her plate with a full house of children, an alcoholic husband, and some real psychological problems. I truly believe like most parents, my parents tried to be good parents. They just brought a lot of their childhood pain into their marriage and children's lives.

As a young girl, I can remember feeling unloved by my mother. I never remember her hugging me, kissing me or telling me she loved me. I never really understood why she didn't love me. However, as I looked at the relationships she had with all her children I realized she wasn't capable of loving any of us. She was very shut off from real emotions and pride in her children. She married a man that took away the emotions that she could not show; his mechanism of burying the hard emotions was by drinking to excess. My father was a funny man, with jet-black hair and sky blue eyes. He was a hard worker that tried hard to provide for his family. When looking back as an adult, I can now see that he wanted to be a good provider and a good dad. He just did not know how.

When he was a child his father, who was also an alcoholic, abused him. He was not taught how to show any type of real fatherly love and compassion. He would drink to numb the pain and then he would become out of control, abusing both my mother and his children. Unfortunately, my mother wasn't strong enough to leave him. The abuse went on for years. I remember once as a child after one night of bad abuse at his hands, I asked for God's help. I asked God to take me away from this place and give me the childhood I saw in fairy tales. I asked Him what I had done to be placed with parents that didn't love me and hurt me. As a child, we went to church every Sunday, and Bible study on Wednesdays, but no one in the family lived our lives outside of church, as God wanted us to.

I loved to go to church and bible study because it was there that I got to pretend we were that fairy tale family. My parents would act proud and loving towards my siblings and I. I realized it was just a show so people would not know the pain and abuse that was going on in our home. We were told by our parents to never share family business as they called it with others. My siblings and I knew that that meant we would be beat if we told anyone about the family shame.

I began acting out as a pre-teen and instead of my parents seeing it as something they were doing wrong I was labeled as a problem child. Finally, when I was 14 my mother decided to leave my father. He had become so abusive that the bruises and scars were starting to show and that public perception was being shattered. I don't want to sound like I hated my mother, but I did not respect her for allowing herself and her children to be abused. I wanted her to protect me, love me, as well as, herself, enough to not allow the behavior to keep happening. We were losing our home because my father's business was suffering because of his disease. The cars were being reprocessed. My mother was really struggling to figure out what she was going to do with 5 children and no real schooling or job history under her belt. She began going out until all hours of the night "cheering herself up" she said. One morning my sister and I got up to a man standing in our kitchen in our fathers' robe. My older sister asked," who the hell are you?" The man said, "you will need to talk to your mom about that!"

Within a week this man was living with us and we were all moving to California from Arizona. We were so confused, but we were glad to no longer be under the abusive hands of our father. Our mother, who would hit us when she was upset, had stopped doing so after my father left. But now this strange man that we didn't know, was living with us and we were moving away from all our friends and family in AZ. My mother had filed charges of domestic violence against my dad and we were asked to give statements. After that my father was unable to see any of us. He didn't fight us on moving to CA because, I feel anyway, he was so embarrassed by everything going on he just let us leave.

It was again at that point that I felt unloved by my father. Why didn't he care if we left? Why did he just give up and not try to get help so he could still see his children? Then there was the pain of my mother bringing a man we did not know into our lives after we had been abused. I remember in the beginning I did not sleep well for fear of what this man may do to me. After we moved to CA, my older sister who had always been a protector to me, decided she could not live in CA. She hated my mom's boyfriend and she missed her friends. She had graduated from high school at this point and decided to go back to CA and find her way. This left me to take on the challenge of raising my younger siblings.

My mother became pregnant by her new boyfriend and was very sick because she was in her 40's at this point! I had to step up and be a mother to my siblings. I had to feed them, get them to school, bath them at night and love them the best I could. It was at that point I realized that I had a gift with children. That I could calm them and get them to learn. One of my younger sisters was mentally challenged and my mother had no patience for her. I would take my time and show her how to do things. Later in life that experience lead me to work with children with special needs. Finally, at the age of sixteen I got my mother to emancipate me so that I could move back to AZ to live on my own.

My mother and I were fighting all the time and I didn't like the boyfriend. I was sick of taking care of her children. I was a teenager and I wanted to discover my own path and live life. I did end up back in AZ living with my friend's family, going to high school and working full time. It was a challenging time in my life. I was trying to discover who I was and who I wanted to be. It was challenging to be working full time and trying to get through high school. It was then that I began looking for love in all the wrong places. I dated a lot trying to find someone to make me feel loved. At 19 I ended up pregnant and married. It was a turning point in my life. My daughter and the love I instantly had for her took over anything else in my life. I wanted to be the best mother to her and give her the life I never had.

I began going to counseling to work through the abuse that I had suffered as a child and worked through the pain of my childhood. It was after the miscarriage of my second child that I decided I wanted a different life. I loved my daughter's father as a friend, but I had never been in love with him. He deserved to be with someone that could love him. It was challenging to decide to leave and live alone with my daughter. I had no car, was in college, and had a fulltime job. We took the bus everywhere we went. My daughter thought it was fun to have to change buses twice to get to her school to drop her off and then for me to get to work. It was exhausting. I would catch a bus at 5 a.m., drop her off at her babysitters, then take another bus to my job, get off at 4 p.m., take two buses back to pick up my daughter, drop her with her dad and go to school a few nights a week. I was so exhausted and broke. There were times I wasn't sure how I would feed my girl but God always provided for us.

I worked in sales and every time I was on my last dollar I would win a contest at work and have money for groceries. I used to lay in my bed at night with my daughter beside me and think how incredible blessed I was to have her. God sent her to save me and she gave me true purpose in my life! As an adult, I faced challenges but none of that really mattered as long as I had my family. I met my current husband in 1997. He was a very loving man that showed me that I didn't need to walk around my life waiting for the next thing to go wrong. We ended up with two beautiful boys together and he had a wonderful relationship with my daughter; life was good for many years. Then suddenly, as life does, it faced us with a new challenge. My husband, who had battled a bad back for year's fell from a ladder and landed on a cement floor at work. He was told he would be disabled for the rest of his life. After four back surgeries, one of which nearly took the life out of him, we got him back to what the surgeons call "as good as it was going to get." We decided we had to make some real-life changes.

I went from working as a teacher with the local school district to working as a director of an early childhood preschool. We were barely making ends meet but I was so passionate about the job I was doing, it was worth it! As I continued to grow with my company they asked me to relocate with my family to Kansas and it was an opportunity to move up in the company. It was a real challenge, but we decided to take the chance and move. It was life changing for my family. My boys were in junior high and high school. We left our daughter in AZ because she was an adult and wanted to stay, but within 8 months we knew we made the right choice. The boys had made friends and were in a good school. I worked for a company I loved, and John was going back to school to learn a new trade he would be able to do with his new lifestyle/ limitations. Life was good; we were happy and content. It was a challenging time but we made it through it and we came out more blessed than we ever could have thought we would.

One of the toughest challenges was yet to come. The company I loved asked me to once again, pick up my family and move, only this time to Dallas. My family had just moved a few years before to Kansas. My boys had a tough transition moving from Arizona leaving all their friends and family behind. But they had just started feeling completely adjusted to our life in Kansas, and now I was asking them to move again. I went to my husband John and said, "how can I ask you to do this again' and he said to me "Baby do you believe in Little Sunshine's and where the company is going?" "Yes", I answered. "Then as you have always told me "anywhere we are together is home, we will make Texas home."

Once we arrived in Texas I was so busy I could barely breathe. I didn't have time to think about anything apart from my work. I would work long hours and dread going home. Every night when I went home to my boys they were miserable. They didn't like their schools, they missed their friends and everything was so different. They were angry all the time and of course they were the angriest with me. My youngest son was having horrible panic attacks and was very depressed. I remember one day I had finally had enough! I went in my room with a pint of ice cream and got in my bath tub to have a good cry. I was praying and asking God why he had brought me this far? How can something I know is so right make my family so miserable? Couldn't my family see I was doing this to give them a better life to make sure I could provide for them! I took out my Bible and opened it to one of my favorite scriptures "have not I commanded thee? Be strong and of a good courage; be not afraid, neither be thou dismayed: for the lord thy God is with thee where ever you go." Joshua 1:9

The next day I went to my boys and told them that I felt God was calling us to Texas. That I would prefer them to stop their complaining and understand that I have a big job to do! However, I have also always promised them that they are number one in my life, and if they were really that miserable, then we would leave Texas and I would leave Little Sunshine's, even though I feel that we have been brought here for a very important reason.

Later, that evening the boys came to me and said, "Mom we don't want you to leave Little Sunshine's, we will stop complaining and support you". From that day on the boys stopped complaining, everyone mentally accepted the transition into our new life and we even started enjoying parts of Texas!

That life change made me see a few things. One, if we truly trust God we must trust him with everything he brings into our lives. Not everything is going to be easy, not everything will always go as you plan, but you must look at each challenge as an opportunity to grow into a stronger person then you were the day before.

As I look back on those times now I realize that making that change in our lives was hard, but it taught the boys something too. It taught them to embrace change, to not be afraid of new things, and to love wherever they are in their life, wherever that may be! I would like to think as my teenage boys grow older they will be quicker to make a big life change and they will be more adaptable well round adults. When I think back on all the different challenges I faced in my life, I know that God needed me to face those challenges to show me my life plan and purpose; to guide me to the places and to the people He needed me to touch or to be touched by!

Staying motivated when things don't seem to be coming together is a challenge at times. How do you motivate yourself? What would you advise someone else?

When life brings you challenges you must see them as opportunities to grow. I always go to God first with all challenges. I pray when things are good and I pray when things get hard. I trust that God has a plan for my life!

My husband John is my greatest support system. He sees the value in every challenge. He loves me no matter what; and he backs me up and believes in me. Having a good partner in life really helps to keep you centered. That partner doesn't necessarily have to be a husband. It can be a friend, a family member anyone that always has your back and supports you no matter what. I have found through the years it is very important to have empowered women in my life as well. I don't think anyone can truly understand the way a woman's mind works like another woman does. It is important that all of us find women in our lives that drive us to want more, tell us the cold hard truth no matter how hard it is to hear at times. They are women that serve as a true example of strength and courage. I have been fortunate to have many of these very women in my life.

When I was a little girl I didn't have that mother figure in my life to teach me right from wrong, to teach me about God's love for me. When I was 15, I was legally made an adult by the courts. I was working full time and putting myself through high school. One of my best friends' family let me come live with them. She was a single mother raising her three daughters, but she took me in and showed me how to be strong, how to do what needs to be done no matter what, and finally to respect myself as God created me to be. Kathy, or Momma Barraco as I called her, would sit me down and tell me the hard truth and then love me even when I was unlovable. She showed me how to work hard and not to think anyone was going to hand me anything in life. "If you want something then go out and get it. Work hard for it and you will appreciate it more.

Throughout my life up to this point, I have always had those strong women empowering me. In college, my professor Rosanne drove me to not give up school just because the course load was difficult while trying to work a fulltime job and be a young mother. "Hard work is what will make you stronger and give you the ability to lead others someday." I have always remembered those words. When I began working positions in which I led others, I pushed them to work hard to not give up when it got challenging to get the job done and not complain! When the opportunity to work for Little Sunshine's came into my life, I was truly inspired by the fact that the CEO and founder was a woman. When I met Rochette this strong-minded woman creating a path of success by building her dream impressed me. Her no-nonsense attitude to business was just the type of woman I wanted to work for! Then, when I met her right-hand gal, I really saw how being empowered by strong women helped drive me to see that if I wanted something I needed to put in the work and learn to take the loses well. Nicole served as a powerful influence in learning to handle myself with style. You have the right to be upset in life but you must always remember to be a lady!

The best advice, I could give other women facing challenges and overcoming them would be put your thoughts on what God wants for you, get yourself a good support system, surround yourself with women you look up to and women that drive you to succeed!

One of the biggest struggles people have is feeling like they are a failure or dealing with failure in general. What are your views on the topic of dealing with failure?

Ellen DeGeneres once said "When you take risks you learn there will be times when you succeed and there will be times when you fail and both are equally important. I agree with this statement completely we live and we learn, we change and we grow.

If life was always easy we would not know how to get up and brush ourselves off when things get tough. Failure is just an opportunity to grow and become a better version of ourselves. When I look back on times in my life when I think I have failed I realized those were the times in my life when I grew the most. Failure is merely just a state of mind. There is no prefect person in this world. We are all merely living our lives to the best of our abilities and finding the blessing in every failure.

What advice would you give to someone who is ready to reclaim and live their sparkle?

My advice to anyone looking to reclaim and live their sparkle is don't let anything or anyone stop you from reclaiming your life. God's gives us only this one life to live it is up to us to live the best life we can!

Living your sparkle to me means, living life to the fullest of your ability letting the light from within you sparkle so bright others want to sparkle too! When we as women reclaim our power, we reclaim our purpose. There is power in a sparkling woman, when a woman enters the room and truly knows who she is there is nothing she can't do!

Only you decide how to live your sparkle. As you walk through life people will try to bring you down and dull that sparkle. I say sparkle on if your light is shining too bright for others that is their problem not yours! When a woman truly knows who she is the pleasing of others holds no value to the pleasing of ourselves. Decide who you are going to be and don't let anyone dull your sparkle!

What "must have" resources would you recommend someone use daily in keeping focused, motivated, and encouraged?

My must have resources daily are my Bible and the prayers that follow me throughout my day. I speak to God so many times in a day. I pray when I am happy, sad, angry and confused. I pray for myself, my family, my friends and for strangers. My true belief is if the world stopped to pray for each other in all things what a wonderful world this would be. Another must have resource would be music. I need music to carry me to a place where I can rejoice, where I can be sad, where I can escape the parts of life that make me doubt myself or feel I am not enough for myself, my family, my job and my God. Music gives me the pure delight of enjoying the beat, singing the words and even dancing in joy and blocking out everything else. Sometimes as women we are required to wear so many different hats. We have pressures placed on us from every single avenue of life. We think being sad makes us weak, I say being sad or angry is to be human. Sometimes we need that good cry, that major melt down, that happy dance to remind us that we don't always have to be super women all the time! We can just be a woman with doubts, fears, sadness, happiness and everything in between.

Please share 5 of your favorites scriptures, quotes or poems that you have referenced when you needed encouragement.

"If God is for us, who can be against us?" -Romans 8:31

"God's people are blessed to bless others". -Zechariah 8:13

One person with passion is better than 40 who are merely interested. -Tom Connellan

Doing what you love is the cornerstone to all happiness! Chose a job you love and you will never have to work a day in your life.- Confucius

Don't wish for it, work for it!

The happiness of your life depends on the quality of your thoughts. -Marcus Antonius

What makes you a woman that is an overcomer?

What makes me an overcomer is that no matter what happens to me in life. I chose to never give up and always look for the blessing in all things. As a child, I grew up in home with an alcoholic father and a mother with mental illness. Many people assumed because of my upbringing I would turn out the same or worse than my parents. I decided that God controls what I become and how my life should be. Overcoming the path and history of my parents was the first time I overcame something in my life. It took strength and commitment to be who I knew God created me to be. To overcome the life my parents chose for themselves, took great strength.

The next time was when I became a parent myself, I overcame the fear of turning into my parents and of not being the best mother I could be. It was then that I truly discovered how to overcome in life! When you overcome something, you take back control over your feelings and thoughts on whatever that it may be. I believe that when you chose to overcome life you make a choice to become what you want to see in yourself and what you chose to become. To be an overcomer you make a choice to rise up, conquer the world with conviction! Take the good days and make them better, take the bad days and see the lesson in that day. Being an overcomer means living your life to fullest each day and enjoying every moment.

As woman in my 40's I have learned that being an overcomer means being in control of what happens to you. By having the confidence to love yourself despite what others may say lets you take back your power! When I decided that I knew who I was and what I brought to the table; I discovered I was not afraid to eat alone! Being an overcomer to me means being able to overcome what life brings and taking the days as they come.

REBECCA BERGMAN

Hello! Please call me Ms. Becky. I am a proud wife and mother of 3 children. My twenty-five year old daughter lives in Phoenix, Arizona, where I was originally born and raised. I have two boys, Johnathon is 20 and Bryan is 16. I have been married to the love of my life, John, for over 20 years. I have been an early child educator for the past 25 years, working in both the public and private sector of education. I have a great love and dedication to the field of early childhood education and believe that we need to love children when they are very young to set the foundation for the rest of their lives.

I started with a private preschool company in 2011 as a teacher and was quickly promoted up to director of the school. In 2013 I was relocated to Overland Park, Kansas to become an area manager. In 2015 I was then promoted to the corporate office as an executive regional manager and soon relocated to Texas to grow the organization in a struggling, competitive market.

Recently, I stepped away from my executive level position to go back to my first love, which is directing a school and making a daily impact on the lives of the children and their families. My true desire in this world is to be a servant to God and to do what I know he has placed me here to do, which is to be blessed and to be a blessing for others. However, as pretty as that sounds, life was not always this easy and it was the many challenges and hurdles I had to overcome to get where I am today.

Email: Beckyrebeccaberg@yahoo.com

Phone: 480-233-6862

Facebook: Facebook/Becky.bergman.58

KIMMBERLY RAMOS

What one word would you use to describe yourself and why did you choose that word?

TENACIOUS - I don't give up when I want something! In fact, I think long and hard before I decide to act because I will give all I have to make things happen. Opposition has never made me back down or settle for less. In fact, it has fueled my fire many times in life. Some challenges you just can't give up on. Having an unwavering spirit can be a gift but, it is not for the faint of heart. I truly believe I would have never overcame some of life's battles without my determination and strong will to not give up and let it get the best of me. I pray and ask God to guide me in what He wants from me and for me in my life. Sometimes, we ask for things that we think we want, but it is not at all what we may need.

Share with us about an experience you faced that challenged you and placed you in a situation where you had to make tough decisions? How did you overcome it?

Growing up for me was very difficult. I never really got to be a kid who came home to any hugs, family dinners, quality time being spent together, and laughter in the home. I learned early on that my life certainly was no fairytale. I had to deal with a lot that made me grow up fast. I came from an extremely abusive childhood that involved physical, sexual and emotional abuse. My relationship with my single mother was extremely unhealthy. Although, the years of sexual abuse were not committed by my mother she knew about them and allowed for it to happen.

My mother's focus and attention was always on the men in her life and not me. She was married 5 different times and had many countless troubled relationships. Many who were violently abusive to my mom. Witnessing such abuse and enduring abuse myself, I felt hopeless as a child. There were even times when I was unable to go to school because my mother had been beaten so bad. At six years-old I remember peeking through my door and seeing her laying on the floor in a pool of blood and unable to move. Talk about terrifying! No child should ever have to witness this type of horrific abuse. This was a painful thing for any child to witness and has left many painful scars to deal with.

Unfortunately, this was a regular thing in my home. We lived within five miles of my maternal grandmother and yet my mother had zero relationship with her own mother. Being the only child was very difficult for me. I never had that mother/daughter relationship that I saw so many of my friends have with their mom's. That also meant more time alone in isolation with many of my mom's husbands that she had been married to. So many times, in my life I wanted to sever my mom and I's toxic relationship. Honestly, most would have never even judged me for wanting to be away from my mother because of the severity of abuse I had endured. Most just accepted that type of behavior because that was just who she was. People also turned a blind eye to the abuse because she did have money. I always had the nice toys, nice clothes and jewelry. Mom showered me with things I believe to compensate for her inability to show love. She manipulated me as a young child with material things.

I would cry and beg to live with my aunt, her response would be," go ahead they cannot afford the things I give you". I never left as a child because I was afraid of what would happen to her. My aunt told me recently that as a child when I was with her that I would ask her to take me to the hospital to make sure my mom wasn't there. We didn't have cell phones I couldn't just call or text to check on her. How shaken and filled with worry I must have been to be so adamant that she takes me to the ER. It really came as no surprise to anyone who knew my mother that she treated me the way she did. However, back then no one really turned people in for abuse. You hardly even heard of that kind of thing back in the day. You just did not speak of it. It was mainly just overlooked and most of the time when I did tell someone their response was "that's your momma!" Sad, broken and confused when I did cry out for help most times that fell on deaf ears.

Back then, most of my friends would have never considered me to be a religious person, but I can assure you that I had a lifeline of prayers going up to God to just help me through every day. My teenage years were filled with bad choices and rebellion. Who even cared? I could do whatever I wanted, whenever I wanted. No questions asked for the most part. I had been on my own since I was 16 years old. Finally, at 19 I packed everything up and moved to Dallas. I began my journey without the eye and judgment of a small town. It is there where I finally met my husband and married.

Living life, happy and excited I now had consistency and stability and was creating the life I always wanted. Everything was going great! I had a wonderful husband, a great job, my own home and was finally pregnant with my first child. It was during the end of my pregnancy that I received a call from a private investigator from my small town. I answered the phone that day not knowing years of bottled emotions were about to be brought to the surface. The investigator introduced himself and began explaining the reason for his call. He said," I have just a few questions", and so at that moment for the first time in my life an adult was asking direct questions about my childhood.

As it turned out there were numerous little girls and boys that had endured the same sexual and emotional abuse that I had. Apparently, a young teenage boy and his sister had been abused by one of my mothers' ex's who had also sexually abused me for years.

The young boy had attempted to kill our abuser by shooting him. This young man now faced attempted murder charges, which would certainty include a felony record and jail time. But worst of all punishment for trying to protect himself and sister from all those years of abuse as well from such a horrible person. As I sit there with my child in my stomach, and tears streaming down my face, I was overwhelmed with so much of my past. This boy's bleak future and the future of my child was at stake and I knew this was the time to make things right. I agreed to travel to my home town and give depositions to the court under oath. I never second guessed what had to be done and I was gladly ready to do it! I hung up the phone called my mother to tell her of this phone call. As if the years of abuse were not enough to break one's soul this phone call rocked me to the core.

My mother and I had never discussed any of the abuse from her or anyone else. As part of my trying to move forward I had opted for just burying the pain and the emotions and starting over. Giving her the benefit of the doubt that she was unaware of all of that had been done to me, I quickly learned that my mother did know. I asked mom "Did you know that he had a past and a history of abusing children before you brought him into our home?" Her reply was like my heart was being ripped out of my body. She said, "Yes, I knew but I hope you told them that you would not be giving any statements!" In a demeaning tone, she asked, "What did you tell them?" I replied, "The truth!" To my breaking heart, she knew the truth. She didn't apologize for her abuse or her knowledge of my own sexual abuse.

As like in the past, her only concern was for her reputation. She said to me "How selfish are you? We live in a small town it will be in all the newspapers, our names and the names of our family will be on the news! Then, with that she hung up on me. She showed no empathy for the young man whose life was on the line. All the victims, in my opinion, deserved to be heard and validated! The very thought she would not only show no remorse for me, but demand I stay silent was like abusing me all over again! How could this be? My mother didn't have to sweep this stuff aside to survive like perhaps a single mom might feel they need to do. My mother came from a wealthy family, owned her home, bought and paid for by her father. Our every financial need was met. She strictly did this for her desperate need for love from a man.

The details of this abuse and the details as to why she allowed it to happen are overwhelming and hard to even explain. Clearly my mother needed help long before we got to this point. I'm not sure how things would be in a larger city, but in a small town everyone just looked the other way. I did go and give my testimony about what had happened in my life to save a young man that I have never met in hopes that he could be validated and heard. After my son was born I had some tough decisions to make about whether I wanted him to even know my mother. I was fearlessly protective of him, but longed for a relationship with my mother and wanted her to know him. The desire to show my mother and everyone else that I can do better is exactly what I wanted. I chose to have her in my life and in my son's life. Somehow, I knew what a family was supposed to be like. I felt like I could make that happen now since I had a support system. I believed in my heart with my faith in God I could break the cycle of divorce and child abuse. For three year's we would go for visits to see my mom. Things were still strained between us and we still didn't always agree, but it was better than it had been for all those years.

Then, in 1996 our lives changed again with the tragic news that my mother was diagnosed with breast cancer. How could this be happening now? It was very difficult on us all during that time. You see, my grandmother had just succumbed to the same unrelenting disease. In 1998, while pregnant with my second child my husband got the news that he was being transferred to New England. This was going to be such a great opportunity for us as a family, but devastating news to know we were leaving and she was in such bad health. We were literally moving clear across the country now, and that also meant leaving my mother and taking her only grandchildren away from her. We were already having to help her maintain her home as she really had not recovered from the cancer treatment. I had spent 18 long years trying to remove myself from the nightmare of my childhood and had 150 miles between us for the past six years. How was all of this going to work? So, my amazing husband suggested that she move with us! With lots of praying and more praying that's what happened. Truly sounds like a great idea but we still had so many unresolved problems between us. Neither of us could address any of it without causing more hateful arguments.

My challenge was to show my kids and mother that family comes first! It was so important to me to try and right the relationship and extend grace to my mother. I wanted so desperately to show her that there was a different way to live and love. Those first years were very hard on her and I. It would have been easier to have moved and started my life over than to try to salvage our relationship, but my heart just could not allow that. I was determined to break the cycle of a broken family. The benefits that all of us received from this one life changing decision were immeasurable.

For years, there were good times and bad times that we experienced just like any other family. My patience was tried over and over but God's grace is sufficient. My children did get to know their grandmother and she built a strong relationship with them and loved them differently than she did me, thank goodness. However, I believe in my own heart she also was trying to make up for all the pain that she had caused. It was a blessing to witness the connection that she had with both my son and daughter. She was patient and kind with them. That for me was part of the healing process and I needed to see that! For the first time, I felt and knew my mom would give up everything and everyone for me and my children.

My mother was so talented in so many ways and had so much to offer. I began to see the good in her. Unfortunately, my mom once again seven years later was stricken with metastasized breast cancer. She died within a year of diagnoses. We had only started truly healing those heartbreaks. I'm thankful that I was able through God's grace put my brokenness aside and share the goodness my mother had to offer with my kids, husband and new friends she made in New England. I have no regrets that I made the right choice to forgive my mother and have her be a part of our lives. God blessed me with an amazing family that really did love me through it all. I miss those moments even now of us arguing. So much can be learned through our pain if only we allow it to teach us what we need to know. If I had to do it all over again I would do it in a heartbeat. I know I did the right thing. I pray that on her deathbed as I sat with her day in and day out alone she knew I loved her and forgave her. There is such a release in forgiving. I did my best to correct generations of a damaged family and still to this day I continue to have that tenacious spirit of keeping all my family together. After all, God forgives us daily and shows his love, mercy and grace to us all.

Staying motivated when things don't seem to be coming together is a challenge at times. How do you motivate yourself? What would you advise someone else?

Well, I know that in life it is not always sunshine and rainbows. Everyone will face their own struggles, and will have to endure and deal with their own hardships. I have been blessed with a few amazing friends and a committed husband that can keep it real when I need it! I don't mean to sound like a broken record but prayer and truly trying to hear what God is telling me keeps me on track.

I would say journal your thoughts and prayers and keep prioritizing what you want and remind yourself why you want it. Trying to look at the big picture and not getting all caught up in the details helps. There may be days you must take it day by day, hour by hour and minute by minute. Decide what things are non-negotiable in your life. For me that is my family. After coming from a broken home, it really made me value family even more.

The best advice I can give to anyone when it comes to staying motivated is having personal connections with those that will hold you accountable and speak words of life into you. There may be people who you may have to remove from your life as well if they are depleting your spirit and draining you of your confidence. Your true friends will believe in you and support you and will be there for you through it all.

In your opinion, what does it really take to win live at dealing with life challenges?

The drive to make a difference and live a life that you can be proud of. To make a difference in all things not just your own life but your friends, family and society. I don't mean you must lead a campaign to save the world or be a law maker or activist. But all of us can wake-up and believe we can make an impact right where we are. For all my challenges and setbacks, I have had blessings and grace shown to me. I have taught my kids to speak up for themselves to be their own best advocates. Always remember give grace to others, say sorry when you are wrong or have said or done something to hurt another. We are not perfect but knowing that and choosing to try and make things better makes a difference. It's up to us to decide if we will make a difference for the positive or the negative.

One of the biggest struggles people have is feeling like they are a failure or dealing with failure in general. What are your views on the topic of dealing with failure?

People live in fear because they are afraid of failure. You are not always going to come out on top, win all the time or even mend that broken relationship. I would say nine out of ten times we need to get out of our own way. We tend to create or recreate past failures instead of looking at each opportunity as a new chance to succeed. That's why for me I turn to prayer first and hand the problem or defeat over to God. Then, I look for what lesson was learned in my failure or defeat and move on. Nothing is wasted and with every failure there is a shift that begins to create change to start doing things differently than what has been done in the past. Failure is necessary so we can learn from our mistakes. Lastly, many times our failure is rooted in what people will think and how we will be judged. Let go of that need for approval by others. You are never going to be able to please everyone and do everything they expect you too.

What advice would you give to someone who is ready to reclaim and live their sparkle?

Your self-worth is not determined by others! Don't let what happened in your life hold you back from living life. Having that tenacious spirit really does come in handy and helps you shine through it all. Don't be afraid to speak about your past failure or mistakes. Others need to hear and be encouraged that when all the obstacles are stacked against them they really can turn a situation around and come out shining through it all. Every day is a new day and it doesn't matter what didn't go as planned the day before. Let it go, move forward and just keep taking one step at a time to move you closer to your goals no matter how big or small. Surround yourself with authentic people that fill you and not drain you. Happiness is contagious, but remember misery loves company. Be a light to others to help them see past life's struggles. You may need to just be the one that leads the way.

What "must have" resources would you recommend someone use daily in keeping focused, motivated, and encouraged?

Time for meditation, and quiet time with your thoughts. Not sleep time but actual quiet time. No media just five minutes to connect with yourself and gather your thoughts. I personally pray and journal. Reading scripture that make me feel empowered and songs that are uplifting and encouraging. People all have something that gives them solace. Spend time doing that one thing or in that space that quiets your soul. For me being outside, surrounding myself with nature and just being alone with my dog works wonders and is good medicine for the soul. However, don't eliminate yourself from connecting with others. Connecting with friends who are other positive sources of light will only add to your natural glow. Not to mention just spending time on the phone catching up with a friend works wonders. You know those people who love and accept you for who you are. Acceptance and love is key for people to meet you right where you are.

Please share 5 of your favorites scriptures, quotes or poems that you have referenced when you needed encouragement.

The most valuable quote for me is, "This too shall pass"! I wish I could stress this enough to young people. We often think this situation is a final and our new norm.
These scriptures are so powerful for me:

"But suppose this son has a son who sees all the sins his father commits, and though he sees them, he does not do such things. He will not die for his father's sin; he will surely live."
Ezekiel 18: 14-17

"He gives strength to the weary and increases the power to the weak. Even youths grow tired and weary, and young men stumble and fall; 31 but those whose hope in the LORD will renew their strength. They will soar on wings like Eagles; they will run and not grow weary, they will walk and not be faint." Isaiah 40: 29-31

"Be joyful always, pray continually; give thanks in all circumstances, for this is Gods will for you in Jesus Christ." Thessalonians 5:16-18

Keep the faith. The most amazing things happen the moment you're about to give up.

What makes you a woman that is an overcomer?

I am an overcomer because I have never accepted my circumstances as final. I have fought against society's view, peer views and became more than what some expected. I have taken on lofty tasks and achieved them many times over in my life. I have even been lost at sea with my husband after a jet ski accident and survived. Even with a broken neck, jaw, and shattered right side of my face I still survived. The will of God and the bravery of my husband really handled all of that. God clearly has a plan for my life. I am tenacious and if I have God's will on my side I'm confident I will always be victorious.

KIMMBERLY RAMOS

Kimmberly Ramos is a proud mother of two, devoted wife of 25 years, and she most recently welcomed her first grandchild. After being an at home mom and raising her children, she decided to write a new chapter in her life by opening not one but two new businesses thus, providing her an avenue for her creativity.

She is the sole proprietor of a hospitality supplies distributorship and a cottage bakery in Keller, Texas. Much of her time is dedicated to bringing to life custom cake creations for her clientele. With her culinary artistry, hard work, word of mouth referrals from her appreciative patrons, her reputation has flourished and is gaining well-deserved momentum in the Custom Cake industry.

Kimmberly has been featured in the Keller Magazine, 2017 Wedding Wire Couples Choice Award.

Instagram: @kimmberlyscakes
Twitter: @KIMMBERLYR
Facebook: Kimmberly's Cakes
Website: www.Kimmscakes.com
Email: Kimmscakes@gmail.com
Phone: 401-835-1443

MONIKA GUZMAN

What one word would you use to describe yourself and why did you choose that word?

Ambitious: I would have to say the best word that describes me would be ambitious being I feel determined to succeed and not fail at what I love to do, whether it may be work, a hobby, a sport or being a wife and mom. My mother and grandmother always said to me growing up, if you are going to do something, do it well, do it because you love it, and give it all you have, or don't do it at all. I spent a lot of time with my grandmother who owned commercial and residential properties, and owned businesses. At times, she took me with her to meet clients and bankers, and I was always amazed how she knew so many people. She was well respected, very busy and successful for someone with only a fourth-grade education.

My sweet mom had a different ambition, and that was to never give up. She was the black sheep in her family out of all the four sisters. My mother was beautiful, stubborn and many times would not take my grandmothers money when offered. She always worked hard to make things happen and to care for us. She taught me to work hard, always be my best and never depend on others to support me. It was important for my mother that I knew and learned this at a very young age. I will not lie, there have been challenging times for me, but at the end of the day, I know I must keep going. Doing what I love and having a passion for working as a Commercial Real Estate Agent, Development and Business Broker makes it easier for me. The ambition is in my heart thanks to two brave and strong women who I will forever love. I am so grateful to them, and grateful to Merri Dee a public figure from Chicago, who is my best friend and mentor of over 20 years.

Share with us about an experience you faced that challenged you and placed you in a situation where you had to make tough decisions? How did you overcome it?

Years ago, I can remember my marriage was a little sensitive at the time. Nothing major but as with any marriage we had some issues to solve and work out. So, after years of supporting my husband's career, being a good wife and mom I thought it was time for me to open a restaurant in case my marriage had failed, so that I had something to fall back on. It was something I had always wanted to do being I had always entertained at my home and loved to make sure everyone was enjoying themselves with good food and entertainment.

Looking back the timing to do this was not the best. However, with hard work, it eventually came together and it was a success. My restaurant venue was very busy. I had no idea what I was getting myself into. I met people from everywhere, and made friends just about with everyone. I worked hard 6 days a week. I would come home exhausted, sometimes in tears and literally had no time for anything else except rest. I had lost my focus for sure.

Here is where my challenge and my story started. I do know that some people try to hide their story, and shove it under the rug in hopes of keeping their personal life private or they have a fear of sharing. For some the challenge must be shared to advise others to not make the same mistake. Sharing my challenge, my story and my experience with you is okay for me now because I have accepted it and it has given me clarity. I knew that others knew about the new challenges in my marriage, but they only had bits and pieces and then again sometimes it was exaggerated to where it became comical.

Sometimes it hurt, because I did not want my husband or I judged. But this is not about judgement. It is about staying grounded and being real and how I became the woman I am today. I would like to express it in hopes of helping others to not make the decision or mistake I made by reacting so fast to a hurtful situation. Staying focused is how I try to live my life now before I ever take a step into the unknown. You see, years ago I was a baseball wife married 18 years to a professional athlete who had pitched in the Major Leagues. He was the father of my children, a good and kind hearted man. With his full support and as I mentioned before, I opened and owned a successful and very popular restaurant venue.

On one particular day, I was excited and looking forward to our upcoming evening, and filling our rooms with beautiful guests. I remember this particular day clearly as it was a Saturday afternoon and I was preparing staff and reviewing the reservation list. I remember the reservation list was full and we were booked with an hour of waiting time for dinner for some of our guests. As I sat there reviewing the list, and the seating selection, I remember looking up and seeing a beautiful, thin blond woman I will call "Molly" walk in before we opened the doors for the dinner crowd. I smiled and waved at her. She asked if I could give her a minute. I was delighted thinking she wanted to reserve a table or book a private event. As we sat down near my employees preparing the tables she proceeded to tell me, "Monika you are a beautiful, confident woman and I can see why your husband is married to you, and because you are a good woman, you should know that he and I have been seeing each other and you deserve to know this." She continues, "He sends me roses to my office and he even called me on Christmas to see if I could meet him in a hotel that evening, but I told him I was out of town." She proceeded with many details only I and my husband would know and so I stopped her there. I buckled and could not listen to another word, especially before my busiest night of the week at my restaurant. I was blown away, and speechless to say the least.

The thing is, I knew "Molly" who happened to be married, because our sons played on the same baseball team. Her son was being coached on pitching lessons by my husband. He had coached pitching lessons to several kids in the surrounding cities where we lived. My heart fell and broke that day. I felt humiliated, hurt and knew I had to hold every tear inside and not let her or my employees see me break. I looked over at my manager and told him to please give "Molly" a drink of whatever she wanted. I am still not sure why I said that, but I kindly shook her hand before I left the room, and told her thank you for sharing this with me. I told her, "This man is my everything and my world, he is kind hearted, the father to my kids, treats me very special, yes, many women approach him, but nonetheless, this is between my husband and I, please do not ever contact him again. Besides you are a married woman". I did not turn into the mean woman she probably expected. Instead I was very calm and collective. Or maybe I was in denial and in shock. I can also remember feeling numb.

I walked away from everyone and went into my office to cry and catch my breath. I had a big night and I had to get it together. I was later told by staff she drove off in a luxury car after she finished her martini. I erased it from my mind so, I could focus on the evening. I can remember being very busy which was good because it kept me focused on my customers and not "Molly" the beautiful, thin blond. When I arrived home that evening, I walked over to my husband who was sleeping and placed my hand on his shoulder. He then wakes up and I say to him, "Molly" your friend paid me a visit today, but go back to sleep we will discuss this tomorrow, I am exhausted. By the way, from this moment on we will live together until we figure this out but we are separated". He said to me he did not know what I was talking about and it was not true, I did not want to believe him. I completely shut him out even though I never had any facts nor did I ever get any from her. But it was just her words that kept repeating themselves in my mind that really hurt me.

All I could think of was why was she doing this. I asked myself, if she is married why would she make this up? Why would she walk up to me and tell me everything by putting her own marriage in trouble? All kinds of terrible thoughts ran through my head. I never gave my husband a chance to explain himself, or a chance for him to share his side of the story. Instead I locked up my heart and became guarded, believing her and not him. I can remember I walked away and got into the shower, fell to my knees and cried. I asked myself if this was my fault? Did I push him away by working to much? Was I not giving him enough attention? Was I not working out enough? I knew he was a gentle soul and a kind person, a good husband and father, I knew he loved me and our family, but maybe I didn't do enough. I blamed myself over and over and I shouldn't have. In my exhausted mind, I knew I was done and I had to walk away from the man who I had loved, the father to my children. I didn't know how, and I did not want to break my children's hearts. This was going to be a challenging time for all of us and I knew it.

The acceptance of the turmoil and the mess turned from hurt to anger and I did not turn to God when I needed Him most. How I wish I had, instead I tried to control this myself without sitting still to think things through. I wondered if I did the same, how would my husband feel? I was totally not thinking straight, only out anger. I was hurt and I did the unimaginable of seeing someone else while I was separated from my husband, yet we were still living together. This man I went out with was not a good person and he made my life a true living hell. I wanted to stop seeing him and give my marriage another chance, and it made him very angry that he held me captive in a room and brutally beat me for 3 hours. I ended up in ER with a concussion, Broken Cheek Bone, Severe Vertigo and deep bruises on my body" It was severe and surreal to me. I was not use to or had ever experienced before. I was very naïve and vulnerable and not ready to date anyone. It was one of the biggest mistakes and regrets I will live with for the rest of my life. This was not the way to handle a sensitive situation like mine by jumping into dating so fast and not really knowing much about this person. I was not thinking clearly and I made a bad choice not putting my children and myself first. My husband looked after me after the beating by that other man, and he was very upset. The devastation of everything and struggle was very hard for my husband and I, and after much confusion, hurt and pain for both of us, we divorced.

For the first couple of years, I wondered if marriage counseling could have saved the marriage and our family. Due to my impulsive reaction without thinking the situation through, I spiraled down to a woman I did not like. My strength and my confidence was gone, and mostly I lived with guilt. Thank goodness it only lasted a very short time. It was not a good idea for me to date anyone so fast, and I never should have allowed "Molly" the thin blond woman to get the best of me. Whether it was true or not, keeping both feet on the ground would have been the best decision for me and staying strong in my faith would have given me a stronger and better foundation at the time I most needed it for my family.

How did you overcome it?

I knew within my heart and soul my life was about to change forever and I knew I had to be strong, stop blaming myself and get my family foundation and life back on track for myself but mostly for my sons, So I sold the restaurant. Then had the money from the sale of the restaurant embezzled by my trustee, but I kept moving forward, I didn't have time to look back. Then I went to get my real estate license and received Christ into my heart again and it was the best thing I ever did for my peace of mind and healing. During the healing process, I made many new friends who were amazing and very supportive.

Still separated, I moved to a home near the lake and bought me an expensive mountain bike from one of my real estate commission checks. I picked up mountain biking and eventually fell in love with road biking. I would road bike every day after work to clear my mind and eventually started to enter bike rallies. It is still what I love to do - to feel the wind on my face. At times, I pray and give God all the glory for His favor, my job, good health, and my three amazing sons. It is a blessing I have great communication with my sons, and talk openly about love, hurt, and forgiveness. It was good healing for all of us. But most importantly, forgiving myself was the start of my new life. We all survived it, time does heal, we all laughed again, and we all have a new chapter in our lives. My ex-husband and I both moved on in different directions and both live good, successful, healthy and happy lives. We still talk when it is regarding our sons and their well-being. Co-parenting has been easy and healthy for everyone. I would not have it any other way.

Staying motivated when things don't seem to be coming together is a challenge at times. How do you motivate yourself?

Quite honestly, I motivate myself by regrouping, staying still, praying with faith. I have learned to believe in myself and trust that the challenge will settle down. I may take a long bike ride for 30 miles or more or take a short weekend trip. My favorite way to let the challenge settle is surrendering it all. I am okay and that in itself motivates me.

What would you advise someone else?

To never have an affair. It is never the answer to a struggling marriage because no one wins. Be better and **stay** focused when a battle or bad situation confronts them, to think things through and do not be impulsive or react so fast without planning and thinking it through carefully; Give others a chance to share their side of the story by being a good listener. It is so important to not be so hard on yourselves, because remember that building confidence within starts from forgiving yourself, and forgiving those who have hurt you, it also gives you peace. No one is a perfect human being and people make mistakes, but never give others the power to destroy you, or allow others to intimidate you. Truly believe in you, your inner soul. It really does not matter what background or past you have, it is who we are now and what we represent. Always be your best, and others will see it and love you for who you are, but always stay authentic and true to yourself. Anything is possible when you stay focused with both feet on the ground. Take a weekend trip by yourself, make time to join a charity for volunteer work, make time for a hobby or sport you love or anything to distract you from the hurt. Surround yourself with solid people who love you and those who really know you and feed you with laughter and give you comfort knowing you can trust them.

In your opinion, what does it really take to win live at dealing with life challenges?

I believe to win big we must first recognize ourselves and our gift, because everyone is born with a gift. Always be grateful and never take anything or anyone for granted. We must remove ourselves from bad energy and the negative, and that would include negative or toxic people. It is important to surround ourselves with positive energy and positive people. Not saying our lives will be perfect, because the challenges will be there, but if we stay focused on the positive and finding that inner peace, it will motivate us to stand against the challenge until it settles down.

One of the biggest struggles people have is feeling like they are a failure or dealing with failure in general. What are your views on the topic of dealing with failure?

Failure is our opportunity to come back stronger. Dealing with failure is accepting it. Staring at it in the face and not allowing it to defeat you. Failure has no power. I truly believe we can all overcome it. We must not allow failure to rule our life or we will never be able to move forward. I felt like a complete failure after my divorce. I felt like I hurt those who trusted in me and those who I loved the most, but after I faced that emotion head on, I accepted it. I knew I had to release it and surrender it to God, I felt that I had no power over it and I had allowed for it to control me.

Until that time, I could forgive myself, let go of the guilt, and move forward with my life. I kept sending out prayers and good vibes of positivity out to the universe to open new doors for me. But I knew it could not happen until I closed the door behind me. I kept telling myself there was no failure, only a monster battle and challenge that I had faced until it broke me. But with all honesty, for me picking up the pieces one by one and accepting the monster in front of me, it took courage, faith, love and strength. I was amazed at all the joy I felt within me once I realized that failure was no longer a word that defined me. I had my life back and only I could control it and set the new family foundation for myself and for my beautiful family.

What advice would you give to someone who is ready to reclaim and live their sparkle?

Define yourself and fall in love with you, embrace the experience that has happened to you during your journey. Remove yourself from those who may judge you, or may be mean spirited. Their opinion has no value until you give it value. This is not where you belong. You have so much to offer others when you reclaim your life once again. If we think back to the time when we were a young child and we had so much innocence and not knowing about life's challenges. We all had big dreams as young children and every dream seemed possible. It was pure, and it was real in our eyes and in our hearts.

You can get that feeling again, and achieve anything you want when you turn away from the negative. This is when you will find that inner sparkle again. Truly be yourself, enjoy the laughter and happiness and never allow others to steal your moment of joy. Know your worth and be selective with your choices. Many choices will surface, but only choose the best ones that will fill your heart and life with freedom and will also fulfill your dream to live your life to the fullest. Be honest with yourselves and be willing to change it. We only get one chance at life, why not make the best of it and be empowered.

What "must have" resources would you recommend someone use daily in keeping focused, motivated, and encouraged?

I recommend the bible for staying focused and encouraged. I also have a good motivational book to read next to my bed and reading it daily or whenever I have a sit still moment before going to bed. The book I love and purchased at a used bookstore at the beach 20 years ago is written by Norman Vincent Peale, one of my favorite authors. *The Power of Positive Thinking* it is a book I have read many times over. Another book is by Joseph Murphy, *The Power of Your Subconscious Mind* a great read for sure and I have given this book to many I love and who are close to me. Another resource would be a support group or any positive group who will encourage you to the next level of confidence and focus. Stay motivated with exercise such as walking, jogging or joining a gym. It releases the toxins, keeps your mind and body healthy and a great way to look and feel amazing.

Please share 5 of your favorites scriptures, quotes or poems that you have referenced when you needed encouragement.

One of my favorite scriptures was one I learned at bible study at the age of 10. I remember it well because we made a wall plaque with it and it hung in my bedroom and home for years.

"I can do all things through Christ who strengthened me" **Philippians 4:13**

"For I know the plans I have for you, plans to prosper you and not to harm you, plans to give you hope and a future." **Jeremiah 29:11**

"Do not fear, for I am with you; Do not anxiously look about you, for I am your God. I will strengthen you, surely I will help you, Surely I will uphold you with My righteous right hand." **Isaiah 41:10**

Maya Angelou: You may not control all the events that happen to you, but you can decide not be reduced by them.

Maya Angelou: My mission is not only to survive, but to thrive, and to do so with some passion, some compassion, some humor and some style.

What makes you a woman that is an overcomer?

Purpose. This one word gives me the courage to keep going. I now have purpose in my life again. It feeds my strength, my passion, my fulfillment. I know I have my family that loves me and still needs me, and with this I want to live my life to the fullest without no barriers, and no discouragement. I have a new sense of strength now. I have felt the hurt of divorce years ago, death of a very dear girlfriend from cancer, and have recently felt the loss of my sweet beautiful mother who died in my arms and took her last breath on my neck. It has shown me that life is a series of memories and moments. Some good and some bad. I continue to live and make time to laugh more, feel more, and enjoying the simple things in life make me happy. I can say that the challenges and experiences in my life have truly humbled me. I never take anything for granted anymore, because I know it is only a moment. I have gained so much from staying positive, loving more, and embracing things I never embraced before. I have found that inner peace inside my soul. I am an overcomer because I am a much stronger woman today because of my family, faith, and choosing to live my life right by making wiser choices. My big glamorous life was temporarily gone, but I am now in a very good place and a successful working woman doing what I love. I stay focused, positive and surround myself with family and people who I truly love and knowing they love me for me. God is good.

MONIKA GUZMAN

Monika Guzman was born in south Texas, and raised in the suburbs near Dallas Texas. Her love of renovating homes in Texas and Chicago, eventually led to Commercial Real Estate and Development. She is a Certified Negotiating Expert and enjoys working in the Dallas - Fort Worth area with her established client list of investors and business owners. She is a member of CREW, Commercial Real Estate Women, NTCAR, The North Texas Commercial Association of Realtors and Real Estate Professionals. She has served on the board for Child Abuse in Chicago IL. Volunteered for Chicago's Women's Shelter, Volunteer for the American Heart Association, and has donated her time with the Fort Worth Orphanage ACH.

She loves hiking, and is a cyclist who enters rallies throughout Texas.

Email: monika@monikasemail.com

REGAN ADAMS-SNYDER

What one word would you use to describe yourself, and why did you choose that word?

If I had to choose one word to describe myself, it would be overcomer. This is a perfect fit because I have overcome so many challenging obstacles in my past. When I was in high school I had my first boyfriend. He was my first kiss, my first everything, and in looking back on what that was like, I can see how it shaped my future. Young love seemed so perfect, but perfect soon became abusive both mentally and physically. After nine years of this and our off and on again relationship, I became pregnant and had a baby girl. Nothing really changed. When we broke up he became very controlling.

Share with us about an experience you face where you had to make tough decisions? How did you overcome it?

Several years later I was introduced to the drug "meth" or methamphetamines, and it took my life over quickly. I went from being a user to cooking crystal meth. Each time my daughter stayed over with her father, we were cooking another round of meth. This went on for over a year, and in this period, I lost my job and lived on very little, surviving on the child support that came in. I knew that the way I was living was wrong and eventually I would be caught and be in big trouble. Sure, enough on July 13, 2003 I came home to my apartment and the police were there. I was arrested and booked into the Mansfield jail and after a few days, my mom came and picked me up. My daughter was in the car when I was arrested and luckily, they allowed my friend to take her to her dad. My first meeting with my attorney was an eye opener. He told my parents and I that I could be looking at 22 years to life in prison. What??? No way!!!! That's crazy I thought. In 2003, they started busting meth labs and now I was one of them. I told my attorney that we didn't make much, mainly for personal use. I was in shock and my parents were in shock. The ride home that day was so quiet. I could not understand why they were giving me so many years. I was so scared and worried about my daughter. What will happen to her, who will she live with?

We had our first court date January 9, 2004 with the prosecuting attorney and I was offered 15 years in a women's prison. I wanted to throw up. I felt sick, dizzy and angry. I was so mad at myself for doing this; I wasn't raised this way. I came from a good home with loving parents and had never been in trouble once in my life before this. Not even a traffic ticket. How did my life get so crazy and bad that I could end up spending the next 15 years in prison? My daughter would be 25 when I got out.

My whole family was affected by this and I had crushed my parents and deeply hurt my sister. I knew I needed to do something, but I had no idea what to do. My sister invited me to a new church in Bridgeport Texas. It was just getting started and my sister said, "I think you will like this church". We went and loved it. The kids even loved it. She was right, I loved it and the worship was so powerful.

The pastor spoke about forgiveness and repentance, and what it was like to be really saved. I had always gone to church and listened, but never really accepted Jesus Christ in my life. I remember the pastor asking if anyone would like to be baptized. I said, "Yes"! I asked Jesus into my life and what a change it made. Every few months I would go back to court and it was always the same offer – 15 years. I had to attend Alcoholics Anonymous, group and individual counseling. I had been taking drug tests every week and I prayed every night that God would let the attorney see me through the eyes of Jesus, hear me as Jesus would, and that the person on the file she was holding was not really who I was. I was a whole new person from the inside out. I had no more fear, or anger. I held no un-forgiveness for my ex-boyfriend. I was free mentally, but not physically. I had that peace that surpasses all understanding that the Lord talks about.

I had never had that before in my life and you would expect me to be scared and not at peace, but that was not the case. Jesus had restored me and I had a choice to follow him and live, or stay where I was and die. On August 11, 2004, I had my last court date. I called my attorney and he said "Regan, the judge has not taken the 15 years off the table". I said thank you and hung up the phone. I went to court and my attorney wasn't even there. When the judge called my name, I said, "Present." Then my codefendant's attorney came over and said that the prosecuting attorney' had just given me ten years...probation. What?? She did, oh my gosh. I went out into the hallway and cried. I called my parents and told them the good news. I just kept saying, "Thank you Jesus!"

When I look back I could have never gotten through those years without the Lord to guide me, give me wisdom, grace, peace, forgiveness and strength to show me the way. I honestly can say I would have gone to prison had I not made the decision to follow Jesus and give Him my life.

Staying motivated when things don't seem to be coming together is a challenge at times. How do you motivate yourself? What would you advise someone else?

Staying motivated can be hard at times, because life isn't all rainbows and roses. My counselor always told me, "You must learn to live life on life's terms, every day is different with new challenges to face. Some good, some bad". I always think of where I was and where I could have needed up. I pray and talk to God every day. For me staying in God's word is so important. I don't think it would be easy to fall back into my old ways. I would advise someone to stay in God's word and to have a strong support system. It is so important to surround yourself with likeminded people. People who will lift you up when you fall and not pass judgement against you

In your opinion, what does it really take to win life when dealing with life challenges?

In my opinion it takes a strong relationship with God in addition to a firm foundation and support system. I could not have gotten through some of the challenges I faced without those three things.

One of the biggest struggles people have is feeling that they are a failure or dealing with failure in general. What are your views on the topic of dealing with failure?

Failure is such a big issue these days with young people in this generation. There is so much competition with looks, career, what kind of car you drive, the clothes you wear, how well you did in school or your success in sports. I always tell my kids that you're never a failure! Always do your best and be your best, and nothing else matters. Don't worry about what everyone else is doing or what they have, you are the person that God created you to be.

What advice would you give to someone who is ready to reclaim and live their sparkle?

For someone who is going to live, reclaim or live their sparkle I would tell them don't look back, the past is the past. Live every day to the fullest, and don't look back. Always smile and go for it.

What "must have" resources would you recommend someone use daily in keeping focused, motivated, and encouraged?

I would recommend someone have a Bible, journal, devotional and a quiet place to pray. I always have my go-to Bible verses which is also a must have resource.

Please share 5 of your favorite scriptures, quotes, or poems that you have referenced when you needed encouragement?

The ones that I say most often are these:

Jeremiah 29:11 – "For I know the plans I have for you," declares the LORD, "plans to prosper you and not to harm you, plans to give you hope and a future".

2 Timothy 1:7 – "For the Spirit God gave us does not make us timid, but gives us power, love and self-discipline".

Ephesians 6:10-18 – "Finally, be strong in the Lord and in his mighty power. 11 Put on the full armor of God, so that you can take your stand against the devil's schemes. 12 For our struggle is not against flesh and blood, but against the rulers, against the authorities, against the powers of this dark world and against the spiritual forces of evil in the heavenly realms. 13 Therefore put on the full armor of God, so that when the day of evil comes, you may be able to stand your ground, and after you have done everything, to stand. 14 Stand firm then, with the belt of truth buckled around your waist, with the breastplate of righteousness in place, 15 and with your feet fitted with the readiness that comes from the gospel of peace. 16 In addition to all this, take up the shield of faith, with which you can extinguish all the flaming arrows of the evil one. 17 Take the helmet of salvation and the sword of the Spirit, which is the word of God. 18 And pray in the Spirit on all occasions with all kinds of prayers and requests. With this in mind, be alert and always keep on praying for all the Lord's people".

Live laugh and love, I love that one. I love, love, love to laugh, so of course," laughter is the best medicine", has to be my favorite.

What makes you a woman that is an overcomer?

I feel like the things that make me an overcomer are the challenges from my past. I knew I had two options: give up or move forward and be who I was always meant to be. Having a little girl at that time gave me the strength I needed to pull myself out of the pit I was in. I could not stand the fact that I could lose her. I was not going to give up or just roll over, I was going to fight for Hayden and fight for my life.

REGAN ADAMS-SNYDER

Regan Snyder grew up in the small rural Texas town of Decatur. After graduating high school in 1992, she moved to the Dallas/Fort Worth Metro-Plex and began what became a 20-year career as a manicurist. During her time in the beauty industry, she was blessed to work in the top spas and retreats in the Dallas area. July 2015 Regan retired to pursue her dream to become a personal trainer, helping people achieve their dreams to live a happier and healthier lifestyle. Regan has been married to her wonderful husband, Tommy for 11 years and they have two beautiful children, Hayden 22 and Noah 9.

Email: reagansnyder@yahoo.com

STEPHANIE OWEN ALBERT

What one word would you choose to describe yourself and why did you choose that word?

Sunflower. It might be a little unconventional to describe myself as an object, but it's what it represents that encompasses the truest sense of what I value about myself. I was nicknamed "Sunflower" when I was growing up by my friends because I always had a smile on my face no matter what struggles I was facing. You see, a sunflower is resilient, grows under the harshest and most disturbed conditions; yet, it blossoms into a beautiful flower that makes one smile from its cheerful bloom and bright color. The sunflower, however, is considered a weed but that doesn't stop its popularity in brightening one's day in a formal bouquet or as just a single flower. It represents the strength, determination, and joy I try to show others. Smiling always even when you aren't in a good place in your life but still believing you can blossom and endure, grow and move forward no matter what your circumstances or environment may be. I call it sunflower power!

Share with us about an experience you faced that challenged you and placed you in a situation where you had to make tough decisions. How did you overcome it?

I will narrow my experience down to one phrase that best puts my challenge into perspective and opened my eyes, "I am willing to live like this but I am not willing to die like this." I was an only child; divorced parents; raised by a loving, giving, selfless mother who taught me courage, to love myself, and support me unconditionally. My father was quite the jetsetter and adventurer who loved me, no doubt, but not the kind of role model that a daughter would want as a parent with a dysfunctional and self-absorbed lifestyle. My maternal grandparents were my rock. They loved each other with such devotion, and were the template for sustaining and nourishing a strong bond and commitment that a marriage takes with every wink, a soft kiss here and there, and the highest respect of one another.

Now let's fast forward to what brought me to my knees in despair and became my wake-up call. Facing your mortality will open your eyes wider and with a heightened sense of urgency than probably anything one can experience. Before being blindsided by the thought of not seeing my children grow up, being there for them in their struggles and triumphs, living a long life, and seeing the sun rise another day, let me lay the foundation of how I found myself willing to live in an unhappy existence, settling for way less than what anyone should accept. I felt there was no choice. I had lived this way for over twenty years. I was keeping everyone happy which became my ultimate reason for waking up every day and not ever questioning my inner voice, my feeling of emptiness, nor the desire to feel that my happiness mattered.

I was young. I love to love, love to give, and most of all, love to be there for the ones I love. That's what makes my heart sing.

Meeting someone who not only was strong and wanted to share his life with me, yet we were opposites seemed at the time to be the perfect match as we complimented each other's qualities. He was very stoic and reserved and me being outgoing and social, but most of all, he needed someone to take care of him since he had back problems. Within the first year of our marriage, he had his first of many back surgeries. I found my purpose, I felt, loving someone that truly needed me, and I was there to support him.

Soon after our nuptials and before his first surgery, I was verbally, physically and mentally attacked. To give you an idea of the kinds of incidents I experienced the first few months; a blow from behind from a nine-pound object thrown at me by my husband that hit my back knocking me to the floor, continuously being addressed with a term translating to "whore" in English by his mother which was accepted by my husband, to one of his family members threatening my life saying he would kill me, to name a few. Of course, you have that inner voice that protects you, but I was very embarrassed, didn't want to let my family down, and he leaned on me for comfort, love, and to get him through his first surgery which was within weeks of those incidents. I wasn't going to abandon him when he needed me. The more he needed me, the more I felt loved.

I should have heeded the warning signs. After three years of marriage, we decided it was time to have a child. I was seven months pregnant as we made this eleven-hour trip and drove to our home state to visit our families. During this trip, an argument resulted in him abandoning me and his unborn child with no transportation, no keys to our newly purchased home and no way to return home. He stated that it was his home and he was leaving our unborn child and me homeless. Mind you, I was also working full-time, as a successful court reporter, and we had purchased our first home together. In his eyes, his unborn daughter and I were dispensable.

I became numb to the obvious hurdles of dysfunction. One of the most egregious hurdles came from his mother calling our newborn daughter a curse and punishment from God for being born with a cleft palate. They looked at it as a defect and wanted nothing to do with her. His reaction regarding his mother's horrendous comments about his daughter's cleft palate showed indifference to our family and acceptance to his mother's appalling claims. This superseded any other incidents that occurred in the marriage no matter the gravity; physical, mental, or emotional. Nothing could ever erase the memory of hearing those words and the sick feeling I had in the pit of my stomach.   We became distant as a married couple.

My mother eventually stopped coming to visit because she couldn't take it. I must say, he loved the only way he knew how. I knew he couldn't love me the way I was taught to love. Love is love, right, no matter how one shows it? If it's all one knows then is that enough? Is that acceptable? I looked at it as though in his eyes he is showing me the best way he can that he cares. I WAS WILLING TO LIVE LIKE THIS. I had empathy, sadness, and wanted to show him I understood by loving him no matter what by being there and taking care of him.

So, what changed my perception, my life, and my tolerance? I had always been in great health. Then I found a spot and it was diagnosed as nodular malignant melanoma which is a rare and aggressive form of skin cancer. Three months after finding the lesion, I had it checked. When my doctor called with the results it was very serious. The doctor said," you have a fast-growing form of malignant cancer and we have scheduled you to be seen as soon as possible by the oncologist at the Emory Cancer Hospital". Within a week, I had been seen by the oncologist, had the lymphoscintigraphy performed, and was on the operating table for removal of lymph nodes and the tumor. I was still stunned. In the back of my head, I either did not hear or understand initially the word "malignant" and still didn't comprehend it until after surgery.   I returned home with a five-inch incision on my arm and two-inch incision in my armpit. They didn't know if they had gotten it all, and I was being monitored closely for the first few months. I was very lucky to have caught it early enough since it was an aggressive form.

As the doctor stated, if I waited three more months the prognosis would not have been favorable. So, waiting at home to see if another surgery was forthcoming was the longest six months of my life. I was in agony and my emotions were so raw.   At that point in my marriage, I was sleeping on the couch as he stated many times it was his house, his bedroom, his car, etc. After surgery, I wasn't even offered the master bedroom as I was recovering. I was treated as though nothing was wrong. My sanctuary was the bathroom where I would cry in the shower or bath. He would bang on the door and demand for me to get out of the bathroom because I was in there too long and he needed to get ready for bed. We had more than one bathroom that he could use. Just another indication of how much I didn't matter and how he had no sympathy nor tolerance for my health much less not even worrying about the possible outcome. He was just annoyed and was complaining that things weren't getting done according to his expectations around the house and his needs. It was all I could do to just keep up with my children's needs and the basic needs of the everyday chores as well as working part time, of which the doctor had said no stress and to cut back on any exertion to heal and keep my immune system as strong as possible.

At this point, you can't pretend that everything is okay. Your children see your value in the home, your value to your partner, the value you give to yourself. When you realize, your children are watching and not do anything about it, you let someone else define your worthiness. Having no support, no empathy, no physical or emotional concern from my husband set the tone for what my children would accept and allow in their own relationships. I was willing to live like this, being ignored, used, treated as a servant, not respected, talked down to, disregarded, not an equal, but I was not willing to die like this, thrown aside, not cared for, looked down upon. My life meant more. My children deserved to see this was not their destiny to accept when making their choices in life. I was showing them that this type of marriage or relationship was okay by staying and, if I had relapsed, I was showing them it was okay to die in a situation like this.

You can ask yourself are you willing to live this way but your future and the way you look at life changes when you ask yourself are you willing to die this way. When I was cleared of cancer after one of the critical time periods of two-years, I filed for divorce. No, I wasn't willing to die like this, and I was strong enough emotionally and physically at that point to not accept to live like this as well.

Staying motivated when things don't seem to be coming together is a challenge at times. How do you motivate yourself? What would you advise someone else?

Staying motivated is the key to growing, learning, and moving forward in life. I can honestly say that was one of my hardest obstacles. Some days I felt so defeated. I felt broken and thought I didn't have the strength to get through another day. Feeling true despair, ashamed of being sad and beat down, and I didn't want to burden anyone with my struggles. This was so unlike me. I had always been the positive one. Being my cheerful self and showing the world on the outside that everything was perfect in my suburban cookie-cutter family. Then the moment of truth and harsh realization that what I had avoided and created was a house of cards so fragile that it came crumbling down when I couldn't keep the perfect image up and that our little world was anything but happy or normal.

It took being diagnosed with cancer that led me making a place for me in my life. I couldn't be everything for everyone like before so I had no choice but to confront head on that I was living a lie of bliss and happiness seen from the outside as truth but it wasn't. There are people that thrive on beating you down, making you cry, and taking away your self-worth. I stood up for those who went through hard times, and supported them. I didn't even realize how much in denial I was about my own circumstances and learned to live with it. It took being faced with my mortality to open my eyes, see past this dysfunction I had been living in and forced me to forge a new path that allowed me to see that I was worthy to be taken care of and loved.

The hard part was just beginning. Standing up and believing in myself was the biggest mountain I had ever climbed. Going through a divorce demanded that I put myself first, something that I was not used to. I lived to make others' lives comfortable and happy. That's what made my heart full. I had to relearn how to live my life by looking forward to each day and including me in it. This including what made me happy, putting me in the equation of importance equal to those that I took care of and valued. I had to make me worthy of happiness and fight for it.

It took a long time to motivate myself to not live for others first and move forward every day for me which made everything else fall into place. I had to give myself that time to cry, be sad, feel those feelings of loss just like you feel joy. It's being human, having a chance to heal, validating and acknowledging that what you feel and experience is important and real; cry for you, grow for you, enjoy for you, heal for you, and LIVE FOR YOU!

I learned it's okay to make room for me and would find myself smiling out of nowhere because I felt like smiling for me because I was happy. The most content moments are when I've found myself treating my inner spirit and joy as my first priority. In that moment thinking, "wow, it didn't take away from giving to others or taking care of others and let me feel joy by taking care of me". I had more to offer as far as living an authentic life which showed my children that you can overcome, love yourself, and still be there for the ones you love. So, what motivated me was recognizing when I was at my lowest, I gave myself permission to feel the emotion, and then reminded myself that it is only temporary. You are not losing but winning when you acknowledge your feelings, let yourself feel all your emotions, and realize you are human and this, too, shall pass.

In your opinion, what does it really take to win at dealing with life challenges?

Understand that it's all in your head. The world is neither with you nor against you. You must change your way of thinking. Stop letting others minimize your worth. It is completely up to you how you want your mornings to begin and your days to end. You can either make your life a living hell day by day or you can STAND UP for yourself, change your perspective, and live a happier life because you choose to not let anything or anyone choose it for you. I realize that it is easier said than done. I have been there. Once you practice letting go of the negativity that is thrown at you by those that are unhappy or those that gain from your misery and not take it personally; but treat them as the ones that are really struggling, that's when you can live your own truth and be happy in your life.

I learned in my divorce that no matter how hard I tried sometimes I couldn't control every decision that was unrightfully made, every act someone hurt me with, nor every effort to diminish my worth. So, letting go and moving past the nonsense and spending my energy on what deserved my attention and time was a healthy choice I made for myself. It doesn't happen overnight. I had to relearn how to live for me and not let someone else define me. The giver puts the dysfunction ahead of themselves and thinks they can change the outcome. It doesn't work. What you allow people to do to you, they will continue to do to you. When you take back control of your self-worth and listen to your inner voice, you win and the prize is peace.

One of the biggest struggles people have is feeling like they are a failure or dealing with failure in general. What are your views on the topic of dealing with failure?

I don't like the word "failure" because failure and success go hand in hand and what makes us evolve and be better spiritually, individually, and economically. No one is born perfect nor with all the answers so failure is inevitable and with that brings problem-solving and innovative ideas to create success. It also teaches by example that never giving up and overcoming those bumps in the road are what life is made up of. Life isn't made to be easy. It's made to be unforgettable, challenging, adventurous, joyful, unpredictable ... life is made to be lived! You are not a failure ever. You're just like the rest of us, imperfectly finding your way through trial and error. Bring it on, life!

What advice would you give to someone who is ready to reclaim and live their sparkle?

I lost my identity, my own way of thinking, and my voice. So, my advice to anyone would be at the end of the day to be your true self, honor your divine path, and listen to your inner voice because every second you spend letting others define your feelings, outlook, and purpose in life is a second of happiness you can't get back. Don't be afraid to take chances, love life, help others, and smile until your face hurts. Be your best and take back YOUR SPARKLE! You deserve nothing more than to look back at the end of your time on this earth and know that you weren't afraid to live your life to the fullest each day with the ones that inspire and lift you up to make a difference for a better tomorrow!

What "must have" resources would you recommend someone use daily in keeping focused, motivated, and encouraged?

The resources I couldn't have lived without are my family and friends, journal, and spiritual compass. Surround yourself with those that inspire you, make your heart sing, encourage you to be your best, and you trust to hold you up when you are most vulnerable.

My mother was the constant and anchor to me gaining back my self-confidence, strength, and opening my heart to a new life. She never gave up on me and encouraged me at every turn, was there to catch me when I fell, and believed in me when I didn't believe in myself. She is my hero. I had a small circle of friends I leaned on to get me through my darkest times. Being the only child, I was used to not having anyone to turn to and felt uncomfortable letting anyone into my world because I didn't want to be a burden. So I stress the importance of having faith and finding strength in those that reach out and you feel a genuine connection. I couldn't have gotten through without learning how to rely on my friends whom I cherish to this day.

They were my angels whom I didn't hesitate to call in the middle of the night when I hadn't slept for days and I just needed to hear them say they cared and I mattered. My spirit sisters who didn't judge me and were patient letting me make my way on my own time. When it hurt to talk about my past and I was so unsure about my future, they unconditionally supported me in those moments and carried me through. I believe in being there for others and how much you can change someone's outcome in life and the domino effect it has in those in their lives as well.

Another resource is a journal or just a quick note I would write on my phone, about either a hard time I was experiencing, something that brought me joy, or just words of wisdom or a simple kind gesture that was bestowed on me that I could look back on and find answers to keep moving forward. Your eyes are the widest and you find ways to solve problems when writing down the sad times as much as the good. In good times, you tend to push away the memories that brought you pain and don't fix the problem which always resurfaces again if you don't resolve it. So, giving it its place in your process of healing and acknowledging the problem and moving forward is as important as acknowledging the joyful times.

Lastly, my spiritual self, my faith, one's inner most driven subconscious compass. Everyone has their own path of worship and spirituality. Whatever that may be for you, it will enhance your life, give you purpose when you feel displaced, and inspires the best in you and those around you.

Please share five of your favorite scriptures, quotes or poems that you have referenced when you needed encouragement.

So many have impacted my life over this journey but the ones that resonated the most are:

"To live is the rarest thing in the world. Most people exist, that is all." - Oscar Wilde

"The true measure of a person is how he treats someone who can do him or her no good." -Samuel Johnson

"I have said these things to you, that in me you may have peace. In the world you will have tribulation. But take heart; I have overcome the world." - John 16:33

"And once the storm is over, you won't remember how you made it through, how you managed to survive. You won't even be sure whether the storm is really over. But one thing is certain. When you come out of the storm, you won't be the same person who walked in. That's what this storm's all about." - Haruki Murakami

"You cannot find peace by avoiding life." - Virginia Woolf

What makes you a woman that is an overcomer?

I wouldn't say I have totally overcome and will always be a work in progress to better myself and learn from this experience. I have those moments where I revert to when I felt invisible, not good enough, unworthy, but don't last long. Today, I surround myself with amazing people making my life the best it can be with those that lift my spirits, inspire my soul, and love me for me. I allow myself to keep my mind and heart open because we are blind sometimes to what we think we want and what we need. I found peace and happiness by removing myself from a toxic marriage and being on my own learning to embrace life without walking on eggshells and second-guessing every decision after having my value diminished and just letting myself enjoy a dinner out and other indulgences whereas before those were luxuries I felt guilty having. Eventually, I started to trust again and found someone who I can dream my biggest dreams with, cherish our days together, someone who loves me through my struggles as much as my accomplishments, my soft place to fall, someone I can trust the most fragile part of me, my heart, and still feel safe. He has filled my heart with love. I work on overcoming every day and that is what makes my days brighter, my joys sweeter, and my life happier. Everyone deserves to be respected and accepted for the light they shine in their unique way.

STEPHANIE OWEN ALBERT

Stephanie Owen Albert was born in Texas, the land of cowboys, football, oilfields, southern charm, fierce Texas pride, and where boots are allowed from the boardroom to the pastures. Stephanie is a stenograph court reporter and has worked in all aspects of the field of court reporting including official and freelance reporting, arbitrations, and hearings which include criminal, civil, and family court cases to high-profile trials, taking down depositions and health claim arbitrations, as well as being cleared to work for the U.S. attorneys' office taking Grand Jury proceedings and working in Washington D.C. She served three years on the Board of Directors for the Georgia Shorthand Reporters Association. Stephanie enjoys being a court reporter but has over time become a stay-at-home mom. Really her love is her family and friends. She will always say that her motivation and desire in life is to be there for her family and friends to watch them succeed and be happy being their support to lean on or in helping them in reaching their goals. It is what is most important to her. She admits that raising a family has been more stressful and harder than any multi-party litigation of up to twenty attorneys or more representing the parties at a trial or deposition, that you can leave work at the workplace at the end of the day but your family and friends are where your heart is so every decision you make, every boo boo you kiss, and every tear you wipe away is personal and stays with you in your heart and affects the ones you cherish when it comes to your loved ones, a 24/7 job that she feels honored to have.

Email: sndkgd@bellsouth.net

ALLISON BYRD-HALEY

What one word would you use to describe yourself and why did you choose that word?

The word to describe myself is determined to make a difference and to be the change.

Share with us about an experience you faced that challenged you and placed you in a situation where you had to make tough decisions? How did you overcome it?

A challenging time was balancing being a mother and caregiver for my daughter and son who had cancer 18 years ago. I was a single parent scraping by to make ends met when my son got cancer. I was newly divorced and was scared what the future held. I had the loving emotional support from my family. I also had charities that helped me get my son to Philadelphia to see a specialist regarding my son's cancer. Also, I found other organizations that helped pay my bills so I did not have to worry financially. Fast forward, my son overcomes cancer and my mom gets cancer in January 2011. She passed shortly after and I had to do some soul searching. I decided to make an impact in others' lives by starting a charity to help people with cancer.

Staying motivated when things don't seem to be coming together is a challenge at times. How do you motivate yourself?

I am motivated by many things: love, happiness, inspiration, seeing a difference happening and having wonderful people around me. There are always challenges and sometimes I think it is only natural to want to pull the covers over our head and not get out of bed. WE CAN NOT… life is too short. The weather changes all the time. Sometimes it is cloudy and then sunny. Embrace the sunny days. Cloudy days come ... wait long enough and it will become sunny. My advice is that we all want to give up but hold on long enough and magic can happen.

In your opinion, what does it really take to win live at dealing with life challenges?

How to win is a positive attitude. I TRY!! Not always successfully but if you think and try to get to the finish line on things, one day you will succeed.

One of the biggest struggles people have is feeling like they are a failure or dealing with failure in general. What are your views on the topic of dealing with failure?

Failure is something I think we all fear. I know I do. Examples are: Can I be a better wife? Did I raise my kids the best way possible? Will I be successful in my career? Am I being a good daughter?

What advice would you give to someone who is ready to reclaim and live their sparkle?

Reclaim and sparkle is taking a deep breath and take the first steps. If you see the sparkle in you... others will too.

What "must have" resources would you recommend someone use daily in keeping focused, motivated, and encouraged?

Must have resources are having God be a resource and thank him every day. That is number 1.

To keep motivated, focus and encouraged. I recommend getting up every day and saying to yourself "This is going to be a great day." Trust me I know there are days it can be hard. But when I do that, I think my day goes better because it started off right. To keep my focus, I have a list and that helps keep me on track. The encouragement I get from people around me and reading inspirational things.

Please share 5 of your favorites scriptures, quotes or poems that you have referenced when you needed encouragement.

Quotes I love are:

- You can be gorgeous at thirty. Charming at forty and irresistible for the rest of your life.
- Your mistakes do not define you.
- Don't wait life goes faster than you think
- If it doesn't open. It's not your door.
- Strive for progress not perfection

What makes you a woman that is an overcomer?

What makes me a woman that has overcome? Mmmm… well having two children by the time I was 21, being divorced when I just wanted to be married once in her lifetime, having a child with cancer, becoming a single parent struggling to make ends meet, having failed relationships after being divorced, always having the passion inside me to do more in my life but having to put things aside to try to keep things going for my family. Having to deal with the untimely death of my mom from cancer Taking all that and learn by life lessons.

ALLISON BYRD-HALEY

Allison Byrd Haley is a native Texan. She grew up in Plano with her parents and sister. Allison's caring nature through her childhood lead her into adulthood where she went into healthcare. In 1998 when her second child became ill with cancer she took all her love and knowledge she had to take care of him. By the grace of God, he recovered and for 10 years she raised her two children as a single parent until she met her wonderful husband. In 2011 Allison's mom was given the awful news that she had terminal cancer and Allison for the 3 months of treatment went to every appointment to make sure her mother got the best care. Allison was determined after her passing to always do something to give back. A few years after her mother's passing she started her nonprofit Heavenly Mimi. The blessing of having an organization that can help is one of her purposes in life. Allison believes that we have one life and all of us need to make a difference.

Phone: 469-867-0159
Email: Heavenlymimi4@gmail.com
Website: www.heavenlymimi.org

DEBBIE HEMINGWAY

What one word would you use to describe yourself and why did you choose that word?

OPEN. Characterized by ready accessibility and usually generous attitude: such as (1): generous in giving (2) : willing to hear and consider

Opportunities surround us and many times, they come from left-field. It is essential to keep our minds open to allow the gift of opportunity. With a closed mind, new information is sometimes missed; therefore, opportunities as well. Being open and informed leads to better decisions. Reading, listening to podcasts and staying connected to positive people are important ways for me to remain open to what is happening around us.

"The real opportunity for success lies in the person and not in the job." Zig Ziglar

Share with us about an experience you faced that challenged you and placed you in a situation where you had to make tough decisions? How did you overcome it?

Growing up facing adversity at an early age prepares you for the challenges of life. My childhood home was the first house adjacent to the Sunnydale housing projects. I didn't realize any difference, so in my eyes I had a wonderful life. Resilience and negotiation was learned at an early age.

When I was in the 6th grade the Board of Education, ordered San Francisco to implement a mandatory busing program to desegregate the school system. Students were forced to enroll in schools outside their neighborhood. Every day I rode the yellow bus from the predominantly African American John McLaren Elementary School to the predominantly Caucasian Ulloa Elementary School. Our bus was unruly chaos. No one would pay attention to Miss Johnson when she would yell, "shut the winder." She meant window.

The same seat, everyone took their same seats on the way to/from school. Bullies in the back, scaredy-cats in the front. Each bench seat held three students. My place was in the middle of the bus, sitting between my two best friends, Darla who is Caucasian and Paula who is Chinese. On the way home from school, three notes were passed from behind over our shoulders, one for each of us. "Tomorrow bring me Candy or _____ Money", the note said. Darla promptly checked Candy and passed the note back to Cynthia, Judy and Kathy, the bullies sitting behind us. Paula followed suit. Kathy asked me, "Where is your note? What are you going to bring us?" I said, "I am not bringing you anything." The back-seat bullies were silent the rest of the way home.

When we got off the bus, the back-seat bullies separated me from Darla and Paula, sending my friends home. As I walked home, I was surrounded by the back-seat bullies taunting me, "You think you're bad/tough! You ain't so special! Ching Chong Chinaman!" I ignored them and kept walking. They took my umbrella and kept taunting me. I continued to walk and ignore them. After a while they saw it was no fun not getting any response from me. They threw my umbrella down and left me alone. It was just another night at the dinner table and I did not mention anything to my family about my day. When the doorbell rang, it was Darla's Father with Darla and Paula. He said, "I think these girls owe you an apology for leaving you today. They were wrong to leave you behind when you were in trouble. Friends need to stick together and be able to count on one another."

The next day it was the same unruly chaos on the bus, but the bullies left us alone and no more notes came our way. My friends and I were more aware of the responsibilities of friendship. I had earned the bullies respect and was satisfied with my decision and the outcome.

That year I learned the meaning of courage. This experience taught me to not be afraid and stay true to myself. If you are confident in your convictions people will respect you.

"I learned that courage was not the absence of fear, but the triumph over it. The brave man is not he who does not feel afraid, but he who conquers that fear." Nelson Mandela

Staying motivated when things don't seem to be coming together is a challenge at times. How do you motivate yourself?

Be earnest and diligent in your work. Take time to understand the reason or problem for "hitting the wall" and always remember to "solve the problem." Do not fall into the trap of restarting from the beginning of the process, wishing it was or could be another way. Solve the problem that is causing the delay, etc. Usually the problem occurs after much has been accomplished, so it is unnecessary to revisit the earlier work that brought you here. Don't be afraid to ask for help.

"Be strong enough to stand alone, smart enough to know when you need help and brave enough to ask for it." Anonymous

In your opinion, what does it really take to win live at dealing with life challenges?

I always believed I would have a successful life. One must have faith in their outcome, not succumb to the demands placed upon you by others. Walk on your chosen path and maintain a positive outlook knowing you have you chosen the life you want and work towards it. Be true to yourself and your goals.

People are attracted to confidence. You might not always feel confident inside, but outside you need to project strength. All of a sudden … click, your inside matches your outward confidence. Keep it up and create a habit.

"Daring to set boundaries is about having the courage to love yourself, even when we risk disappointing others." Brene Brown

One of the biggest struggles people have is feeling like they are a failure or dealing with failure in general. What are your views on the topic of dealing with failure?

There is failure along with disappointment and embarrassment. No one wants to fail, but it happens. Think of failure as the first step to a fresh start. Why did "it" fail? What could I have done better? Was it me or the circumstance? Was there a way for me to win "it"? What have I learned? How do I win the next one? Think outside your comfort zone. If you lack knowledge, seek education. Emulate someone who excels at what you are trying to accomplish.

Get uncomfortable and take a leap into the unknown. You may excite and surprise yourself.

"Start before you're ready. Actions create momentum" Marie Forleo

What advice would you give to someone who is ready to reclaim and live their sparkle?

Always remember what you want, focus, go directly from A (where you are presently) to Z (goal). You may not get there overnight, but you will be getting closer to the life you want. If your circle of friends includes naysayers, take a break from them. Surround yourself with like-minded people; create synergy in your life. Remain true to your goal and connect with new like-minded people. Turn to self-improvement podcasts, books or inspirational speakers for new ideas and guidance.

Remember that excitement you felt when you first rode a bicycle by yourself or looking forward to that Disneyland trip? Get into that feeling. Feel excited about the people you are contacting; feel excited about the people you can help with your knowledge; feel excited about doing an exemplary job. There is only one you.

"The gift you have is yours alone, share your gift. Light up and Shine!" Kathy Eppley

What "must have" resources would you recommend someone use daily in keeping focused, motivated, and encouraged?

To stay motivated and focused I use techniques that will fit easily into my active life.

1. Keep a 3" x 5" card with your affirmations or goals in multiple places to read and see often.

2. I listen to podcasts with my earphone when I get ready for work and choose a topic that resonates with me for the day. Some of my favorites are:

- TED Talk Radio Hour
- Marie Forleo Podcast
- Tony Robbins Podcast
- Tim Ferriss Show

3. Write three things you are grateful for.

4. Write five thank you notes a day.

5. My favorite books to inspire and motivate:

- *The Art of Possibility Transforming Professional and Personal Life* by Rosamund Stone Zander & Benjamin Zander. This book taught me to look at things differently. Delightful read.
- *You 2: A High Velocity Formula for Multiplying Your Personal Effectiveness in Quantum Leaps* by Price Pritchett, Ph.D. This book will get you moving into action.
- *The Speed of Trust: The One Thing that Changes Everything* by Stephen M. R. Covey (son of Stephen M. Covey!). Think simply, not complicated.
- *Tools of the Titans: The Tactics, Routines, and Habits of Billionaires, Icons, and World-Class Performers* by Tim Ferriss. Fantastic how-to book covering a multitude of topics within 673 pages. Tim interviews 100+legends; Laird Hamilton, Seth Godin, Tony Robbins, Paulo Coelho, Brene Brown and more.
- *Pretty Good Joke Book A Prairie Home Companion.* Introduction by Garrison Keillor. Sometimes you need to lighten up and laugh.

Please share 5 of your favorites scriptures, quotes or poems that you have referenced when you needed encouragement.

To stay in the right frame of mind, these are some of my favorite quotes:

- "Success is liking yourself, liking what you do and liking how you do it." Maya Angelou
- "Nothing is impossible as the words itself say I'm Possible." Audrey Hepburn
- "Don't be upset by the results you didn't get with the work you didn't do." Anonymous
- "Start before you are ready. Action creates momentum." Marie Forleo
- "People may hear your words, but they feel your attitude." John C. Maxwell
- "Screw it, let's do it." Richard Branson

DEBBIE HEMINGWAY

 I live, work and was born in San Francisco, California. Fourth Generation Chinese American modern woman who enjoys fashion, beauty, healthy lifestyle, connecting with people, a sense of humor, having fun, investing in real estate and helping my clients sell/buy real estate. I sell luxury residential and investment properties for Sotheby's International Realty. To stay fresh after 30 years in the business I read self-help, inspirational books and believe in affirmations. Growing up on the wrong side of the tracks has given me invaluable lessons in survival. My gift is being open so I can connect with people.

Phone: 415-640-1487 mobile – call or text
Email: Debbie@DebbieHemingway.com
Website: http://www.debbiehemingway.com/about-debbie/
Facebook: https://www.facebook.com/debbie.hemingway1

CORRIE WELLS

What is one word you use to describe yourself and why did you choose that word?

Diamond. A diamond is created, it doesn't just start at being a diamond. Jewels go through a process of pressure, heat, and many other adversities to become the precious, vibrant, shiny, and brilliant stone it was intended to be. Without the adversities in our lives we would not have the opportunity to ultimately become the jewel God intends for us to become.

Share with us about an experience you faced that challenged you and placed you in a situation where you had to make tough decisions? How did you overcome?

The experiences that challenged me most was trusting that Gods love was enough to help me seek support to not allow depression to cripple me and to trust God's provision for my life. December 26, 1974, my two sisters and I were at my grandparents in Fort Worth, I remember sitting in the living room and being told that my daddy just died. I was 5 years old and the baby of three girls. After my daddy's graveside service in Weatherford, Texas, we went back to Austin where we lived. It seemed like it was only days after we returned to Austin that my mom introduced a man to me who sat me on his lap and told me he was my new daddy. Ironically, I remember a tee-shirt, (I want to say I was wearing it) that belonged to my deceased daddy that had bold lettering that read "BULLSHIT", thinking back on that time, it would describe the next several years of my childhood.

In the Spring of 1975 only a few months after my daddy's death my mom married a divorced man with five children who ranged in age 4 (twins) to 17. My newly married mother and her husband moved their combined 8 children (5 girls, 3 boys) into a single trailer on a chicken farm in Arkansas. Through the summer months I would start to get adjusted to the farm life and I liked having the younger twins to play with. We had horses, a pony, dogs, chickens including, hens, roosters and other wild animals that would keep us busy when not working the farm. We would go to the bowling alley with my parents who bowled on a league, and at times we loaded up in the station wagon to head over to the drive in. We would spend lots of time at the golf course where my stepfather spent a lot of his days. My mom cooked regularly because there were so many of us, and I remember homemade chocolate pudding, having plenty of potatoes, lots of chickens of course because my step father would kill them for my mom to prepare. The egg foo young... ugh, never to be had again after Arkansas.

We finally got another trailer that my step-father added on to the single one we originally had. We were not so cramped in a single trailer any longer. As I adjusted to living on a farm and all the differences, I also looked forward to starting elementary school. Once school started we would stay busy with different activities; Friday night high-school football games with foot-long cheese-coney from Sonic and most days after school the bus would drop us off at the golf course; and we'd trample through the woods picking and eating wild berries while we waited for my stepfather to finish his round of golf or finish playing a few hands of gin rummy. When he was ready leave, we would load up in the back of our little yellow (Brat) pickup truck and head home to tend to the evening farm chores before dinner.

The Making of a Diamond…

I was six years old when I had my first sexual assault, I remember lying on the floor alone. My sister was there, she went for help, where did she go? Why didn't she come back? Where is my mom? Is she going to come for me? My mom never did come for me, no consoling, no explanation of what happened; I was left alone to deal with and make sense of a terrible situation in the best way a 6-year-old could. My step brother went back to Texas to live with his mother; he was sent away. The assault? Never to be discussed. I was rejected, abandoned, and denied protection that would lead to several years of sexual abuse by my stepfather.

After nearly four years on the farm the two trailers we lived in burnt to the ground. As I walk through the memory I can still smell the burnt air. I can hear the crunch of each step as I walked through the char and ash, I can taste the smoky air as I breath, and I can see my suit covered hands as I pick up and examine the burnt coins we found. My family separated to stay with our friends until my mom and stepfather could find a place for us to live. Eventually the church provided temporary housing, donated clothing, and some household essentials. We moved two more times while in Arkansas before we finally moved back to Texas.

Fast forward to the of Summer 1980. We headed back to Texas, my mom moved us to be near her parents, my grandparents in Fort Worth. In 1982 on my 13th birthday my soon to be ex-stepfather wanted to take me to a movie and dinner. I told my oldest sister about my birthday plan and a few hours later as my step father pulled up in front of the house to pick me up, I see my grandfather's van zooming around the corner and pulls up to a screeching halt in front of our house. My sister jumps out of the van yelling for me to get in the van. I don't know what my sister felt that day, but she showed up to rescue me from her fear of my step father with the help of my grandfather. This was the first time someone would attempt to protect me! My mom never inquired about the activities that night or the fear that my sister had. To this point my mom had still not acknowledged the abuse I had experienced by my step brother, or my step father, her husband.

After my mom was divorced, she bought a house and we moved into our first new house, my mom, my middle sister and me. Something happened while in that house, maybe the hormones of turning into a teenager compiled with the years of rejection, abandonment, lack of acknowledgement of what had happened to me over the past 6 plus years of my life. I was angry, I had no self-worth, no value, I did not know how to say no, I didn't know I could say no, which put me in more abusive situations. I had an awful relationship with my mom, I think my middle sister hated me, and I didn't have a relationship with my oldest sister, who had moved out a couple years earlier and I didn't really have many friends, not the kind that were a good influence or that I could confide in or who would be around during the tough times. The boys in school would degrade me by grabbing or "feel me up" (touching me in places they shouldn't have), the girls didn't like me and I was labeled, called names and if I was asked out on a date, it was only to see if I would "put out." I always felt misplaced. I was sad, I merely existed in my misery of self-defeating thoughts, and engaged in self-destructive activities that would place me in the midst of more bad situations. I was alone, insecure and always felt awkward.

Four months after my eighteenth birthday I got married. I looked forward to not living with my mom anymore. Prior to getting married, I hadn't had a healthy relationship, not with family and I certainly did not trust anyone. I never had a healthy relationship prior to the man I married. I was so desperate to be out of my situation that I went from one bad situation to another by getting married. More trials, struggles, and situations that would keep me caught up in the trap of destruction that involved drugs and eventually alcohol. I was married for 9 years and then divorced when my son was 1 year old.

Fast forward to 2001, my son was in kindergarten at a Christian school. During the evenings at bath-time we would talk about his day and what he learned and one evening, he asked me if I knew Jesus; I had dabbled in the concept or idea of Jesus, I even received him as my savior a couple of times, however I did not accept Him. I did not know Him, I did not have a personal relationship with Him. I don't think I really believed in Him to be honest; I played dress up with the idea of Jesus but never actually felt His presence, His love and I did not believe in Him enough to trust His armor. But on this night my son, he began to tell me how "Jesus died for us mommy" John 3:16. Which is the first bible verse we learned.

I listened to what my son had to say, I would help him with his memory bible verses, etc. I think I may have even said again how maybe there is a God, but that was about it, I was still not a true believer. But there was something about hearing it from my child who was the exact age I was when my life began to change so dramatically.

One afternoon I was visiting my aunt and she suggested that I find a church and get connected with a support group of other single parents. A support system that would provide opportunities for my son and me to get connected with other single moms. Prior to her suggestion, I was still trying to figure out how I was going to be a single mom, even though I had been one for several years. I had various jobs, such as working for a temp company doing office work and headed down a path of emotional destruction. I was experiencing depression, and for many reasons, I was depending on my mom financially. I didn't have a career, or a trade. I was lost, confused, and I felt as though I had no purpose.

I took my aunt's suggestion, and I started to search for a church. I probably went to 25 churches until September of 2002 when the school secretary invited me to come to her church on friends' night. After visiting I didn't feel I needed to seek another church, I felt "connected". I felt like I belonged; and it was the second-best choice I ever made with the first being the birth of my son.

About a month went by, and I was still unemployed. I was lying in bed (I had taken my son to school and went back home to bed), depressed, and begging "God" to let me die; living was too difficult, too much pain, and I had enough suffering. For a few minutes, I remember sulking, wallowing in self-pity, crying uncontrollably about how much better off my son would be without me, no one would miss me certainly not my mom or sisters and I imagined an empty church for my funeral.

Then I felt a calm come over me, as I silenced my thoughts. My tears started to dry and energy started to flow throughout my body. I vigorously sat up on the side of my bed, I stood to my feet and started to stomp on the ground and screamed, "Satan, get beneath my feet, that is where you belong, you will not get me today, I don't belong to you" I put on a baseball cap to cover my messy head of hair and ran out of the front door.

I went to the office supply store that morning to pick up a few items. I was being a little nosy, trying to read one of the invitations in a box over the shoulder of this lively older lady picking up her print order. Of course, I couldn't quite make out what it said so I asked her what her invitations said. In this very loud happy tone this lively woman with a very strong Texas drawl began to tell me about the Oktoberfest they were having at a retirement community in Arlington just a few miles away. I stated how fun that sounded and asked her a little more about it and then ask if I could go to the event and she replied, "well sure you can". So, in October I did. I went to this party at a retirement community. I walked around and I said to myself I wanted to work there. They just happened to have the Activity Director position opened and, I applied. I interviewed and soon after I began a career in senior living, partying for a living, that's what I liked to call it. I kept the seniors busy and social, and it was the beginning to a wonderful career with a corporation that I enjoyed for nearly 15 years. A career I would not have been blessed with if I allowed Satan to keep me in my bed that morning a few weeks earlier.

God, He breathed life into me that morning. He was the energy that gave me the strength to not be defeated and to stand up to Satan. I believe with everything I have become that He gave me that career and it was a divine connection (Jeremiah 29:11). He is the reason I can overcome the adversities of my childhood that I have battled and fought so desperately to overcome most of my life. I think back on how many times I allowed Satan to keep me "in bed" instead of stomping him into the ground. I think about how most of my life I allowed myself to be the victim of the circumstances that I was placed in. How I treated myself as though I did not deserve anything good. If there was a God how could He allow these horrible things to happen to me? Why did I deserve it? Why did I have to be the victim of sexual abuse, and why did I not get the opportunity to have what some would consider a "normal" childhood?

I wasn't nurtured by a mother, nor was I made to feel important by a father. Why wasn't I told how valuable I was? Why didn't I get to learn healthy safe boundaries? I was a recipe for disaster, and as one can only imagine I was not the most mentally stable child considering the rejection, abandonment, and the degrading actions by others to harm me that I experienced. I was a messed-up kid and I grew up to be a messed-up adult. I was sad and lonely as a child, and I grew into a sad and lonely adult. I always felt scared and insecure, like something was wrong with me.

I learned from an early age that I was to comply and not question what didn't feel right. When I was a teenager I was out of control. I was angry and I had an awful relationship with my family. We fought, spoke with anger and we despised each other. The feelings of inferiority continued to permeate in my head and I did not believe I was "worthy." I felt that everyone was better than me; I was broken, blemished, tarnished, insignificant, and irrelevant. I did not understand that what I survived was unhealthy mentally, physically and emotionally. I believed I deserved all the bad that I had endured as a child, and I would continue to make decisions that would keep me down even as an adult.

I wanted good things in my life, but I didn't understand how to receive them. Once I believed I was worthy, and deserving I could understand that the "stuff" I experienced growing up did not define me but the relationship I had with Christ defined me. All the bad things didn't happen to me because I deserved them, but because of bad people in my life. Like a lump of clay, the adversities I have faced are what molded me to become who I am today; a successful, healthy mom of a grown son and the grandmother of a beautiful baby girl, who loves Jesus with all her heart, all her soul and all her mind.

I could overcome my circumstances because I allowed myself to believe in what Jesus did for me. I believed that I am deserving to receive all the desires of my heart and that He has a plan for my life. I am worthy and I am loved by a Heavenly Father who wants good things for my life. He loves me with all my flaws, failures - despite my sins. I have the faith to believe that I deserve every good thing that this life has to offer me, including loving, faithful, loyal friends and healthy, and respectful relationships.

I loved my career that was provided to me as a divine gift from God, one that I had been able to be successful in and that allowed me to serve others every day. I have a wonderful son, who is healthy, a hard worker, and a wonderful daddy to his precious daughter. I know the example I set for him growing up has helped define and mold him into the man he has ultimately become. Even though we struggle in our relationship, I know the choices I made to improve myself for his best interest will be the motivation he needs to do the same for his daughter as she grows into a beautiful young woman.

Staying motivated when things don't seem to be coming together is a challenge, at times. How do you motivate yourself? What would you advise someone else?

The motivation I have is sometimes driven by others and my desire to create in them something they didn't realize existed. I never wanted to be a career women. I didn't want to be the breadwinner in the family. I wanted to be a wife and mom, but in an ironic twist of circumstances; the driving force for me was my son. I had no other options or choices; I was going to raise my boy alone and that required me having a career, with the anticipation of raising my son to be a productive adult who would be a contributing member of society. I had to consider what I needed to do to raise him.

I wanted him to grow up to be a good father and a good provider for his own family one day. I made the sacrifices to do what I needed to do to create the healthiest childhood for my son that I could. I wanted to protect him from the brokenness of my own childhood. I know that when times are challenging "this too shall pass" even in the depths of my sweat, tears, and frustration. When it feels like I am the only one on a mission to complete a task I look to God to be my strength and when it feels as though I am the only one going above and beyond to make it work, I rely on God to be my motivation. Also, motivation comes from the thought of the relief, or idea of final satisfaction, and thinking it is almost over, and imagining that breath, the sigh, the gasp, or the final exhale. I think sometimes we all struggle with being motivated because of challenges and in those times, ask yourself, what does the result look like? "Motivation shouldn't be difficult to find when you have a clear picture of the end in mind."

In your opinion, what does it take to "win live" at dealing with life challenges?

To "win live" is the desire to glorify God while allowing Him to navigate our journey and acceptance of the divine connections He custom designed to assist us in overcoming the many adversities/challenges we face, have faced will face all while on our way to His kingdom (John 14:2).

One of the biggest struggles people have is feeling like they are a failure or dealing with failure in general. What are your view on the topic of dealing with failure?

I know on my journey that failure is a part of it; we can't experience success if we don't experience failure (2 Corinthians 12:9-10). If you tell yourself, you're a failure, expect to fail. If you tell yourself it is necessary to fail to rise to a new level, then failure has just gained a new meaning. It now becomes a step in the direction you choose. We control our thoughts; our thoughts do not control us. We must believe we deserve everything that God says the universe has for us. We can be our biggest fan or our own worst enemy. What we feed ourselves is what we believe. So, believe God, His word, and His promises (Romans 12:2).

I lived for so long feeling undeserving. I thought I had to earn His grace, but it was His gift to me, all I had to do was receive it. I am royalty, I am the daughter of the highest King and I want to receive all His gifts. If you can see it, it can be yours, if you speak it, it can be yours (Romans 4:17). If you desire it, claim it in the name of Jesus and it shall be yours. For He is the God of love and wants to grant us the desires of our heart (Psalms 37:4).

Remember when we give a thought to what others may think about us, we are giving away energy that we need to keep ourselves energized and motivated. One thing I always must remind myself is "no one will love me as much as me, no one cares about me more than me and at the end of the day, I am the only one in my head" "Don't live vicariously through what you think the thoughts of others are." What other people think about you is none of your business, only what God believes about me is what matters, in Him and only in Him can I live loved.

What advice would you give to someone who is ready to reclaim and live their sparkle?

To shine and be a light to others we must believe we are worthy. It's a gift and we don't have to earn it. I want everyone to know they are WORTHY, valuable, deserving and have the right to receive everything good. Do something today that will positively impact your future no matter how uncomfortable it is, remember, a diamond didn't just become a diamond, it had to be created through a process of pressures and intense heat. Your sparkle is inside of you, but you must choose your shine and what you want your light to say.

I know that I know that God has plans to use me to glorify Him. I know that I cannot be defeated by the negativity surrounding me unless I give it power. I know that it is a daily continuum of improving me to be the light for other that God intends for me to be in His Kingdom. I want to keep learning, to continue to grow in my faith and my relationship with Christ to live loved, and be a beacon of light for others.

What "must have" resources would you recommend someone use daily in keeping focused, motivated, and encouraged?

A few bible scriptures to help keep you focus on God's word and His will for you. Daily prayer, in your car, in your journal, while taking a shower, bath, while on your lunch break any time is a good time to pray. Having friends that are on the same spiritual path as you. Having friends that want to celebrate you and your achievements, regardless of how big or how small, an achievement is an achievement. Self-Talk; believe in your purpose, believe in Gods promise. Listen to Podcasts, YouTube, read the bible, books, audio books, anything that is feeding your soul with healthy content. Turn off the secular radio, plug your life into positive influences. Talk to your inner child, remember you made promises to a little you and she has not forgotten your promise, revisit her regularly, remind her she is valuable and worthy of your promises.

Please share 5 of your favorite scriptures, quotes or poems that you have referenced when you needed encouragement?

"Confront the fear of Knowing Yourself" author unknown

" So, do not fear, for I am with you; do not be dismayed, for I am your God. I will strengthen you and help you; I will uphold you with my righteous right hand" Isaiah 41:10

"For I know the plans I have for you," declares the Lord, "plans to prosper you and not to harm you, plans to give you hope and a future" Jeremiah 29:11

"Call those things which be not as though they were, speak to those things that are not as though they are" Romans 4:17

Let us not become weary in doing good, for at the proper time we will reap a harvest if we do not give up. Galatians 6:9

What makes me a woman that is an overcomer?

I have learned to appreciate what I have been through because it is too easy to regret the past, but what's hard is accepting the past and not allowing it to affect the present or dictate the future. We must go through adversities that ultimately create the jewel God intended for us to be. The adversities I faced through my struggles, heartaches, and general challenges are the events that are forming me to be the jewel "Diamond" God created me to be and I hope to have the blingiest crown in heaven one day but until that day, I will continue to walk in His love, His mercy, His grace, His word and I will walk through the rest of my day living loved.

CORRIE WELLS

 Corrie is a single mom of a 21-year-old son and is the proudest "Glammy" of her 2 year old granddaughter. She enjoys spending time with her granddaughter and traveling. Corrie made a career out of her passion for people and had the opportunity to work caring for others for 15 years for a corporation operating senior care homes. Over the years, she worked her way through the operations of her industry to place herself in a position that had the ability to create an environment that was safe, enjoyable and life enriching for the seniors she served. Corrie has ventured out on faith and her belief of Jeremiah 29:11 into the unknown to build a new career serving others and she is excited about her future and how God is going to use her to serve.

Email: corrieww@att.net
Instagram: @ ntx_lady

YOLANDA CONTRERAS TAYLOR

What one word would you use to describe yourself and why did you choose that word?

TRUE

My life is a journey in search for a deeper understanding of people, our existence, the fine line between life and death, our motives, and relationships. I pressed a very small circle of friends and I believe their responses line up with "True." Loyal and sensitive applies to being a true friend. Convinced and determined is living true to my core convictions. Deep and a thinker is remaining true to my mind. Lovely, funny and loving is living true to my soul.

Share with us about an experience you faced that challenged you and placed you in a situation where you had to make tough decisions? How did you overcome it?

SHOCK AND AWE.

I was diagnosed with breast cancer four years ago, in late June of 2012. Prior to that, I had been closely followed by my breast surgeon for 10 years. At the time of diagnosis, the tumor was identified as a triple positive and a high grade "sneaky fast grower."

I had never considered myself a prayer warrior, so I was quick to recruit those who expressed their gift as "life happened." Ironically, my 2012 spiritual New Year's resolution asked God to teach me how to pray.

The call from my surgeon came in at 5:37 pm on my way home from my volunteer work at a children's clinic. I listened carefully as she confirmed what I already knew in my heart. It was cancer. We would meet the following afternoon to discuss a plan of action, Yolanda's treatment course; my life in outline form for the next six months. I remember hanging up as tears welled up in my eyes. I also remember praying, settling on three thoughts: the truth that I had been bought at the cross by my Lord, Jesus Christ, my life was not my own, and my hope that I would be counted worthy of this calling to His Glory. I had no idea what that meant or what it looked like, but it continued to ring in my heart and was shared in each discussion I would have for the next several days.

It was not that our hearts were not broken. In fact, it was quite the opposite. When I was finally able to share the news with my husband, Jim, I was met by unexpected anger. I had waited until we were finally alone in the car on our way to pick up some take out for dinner, at which time he asked, "When were you planning on telling me?"

As he led us into prayer, I listened as his heart transitioned from the heartbreak of an unanswered prayer to one of faith, trusting God's plan as he had our last 25+ years together. I shared my prayer experience that encouraged us to run with endurance the race set before us, looking to Jesus, the founder and perfecter of our faith, who for the JOY that was set before Him endured the cross..." (Hebrews 2:12); and, reminding ourselves that He had given THANKS..." (Luke 22:19).

Life had delivered several opportunities to practice: a child diagnosed with autism, the loss of an unborn child, the loss of a loved one to a drunk driver and recently, a parent diagnosed with Alzheimer's. With our children, now of an adult age, we made our decision based on one factor: survivability.

What does that look like? For Jim and I it was complete elimination of anything that could possibly be an opportunity for cancer to make a return appearance. These GURLZ were DONE, so minimally, a double mastectomy. Our faith told us that our loving

Father had already selected the team needed to fulfill what was needed, and the countless prayers of family and friends followed. On Friday the thirteenth, around noon, I was wheeled into my OR after a time of prayer. I later found out that the waiting room held prayerful family and friends, many of whom I would never see that day. My husband and family were astonished at the love and courage each poured into their hearts. I'm beyond grateful for the skill and kindnesses the team bestowed in my care. The surgeon, the anesthesiologist, the plastic surgeon, the nurses, the medical assistants. God is good. All the time.

"OH, I'll GET BY WITH A LITTLE HELP FROM MY FRIENDS": DRUGS.

I am not myself when they are in my system. There's nausea and vomiting. Communication is nearly impossible with the drug induced narcolepsy. I was desperate to have my mind back. I had lost my ability to spiritually process what was occurring. Drawing closer to God was my highest need and priority. I was off the narcotics within two weeks. Being open with my struggles allowed "my team's" insight work towards my benefit (Jeremiah 29:11). My loving sister-in-law arrived and appreciating my less than normal mental capacity, introduced me to a book. Chris Tiegreen, author of *"The One Year Wonder of the Cross Devotional,"* offers a single page read utilizing scripture, relatable insights and a quote that lands a punch of conviction. Every day my focus was on the cross. That is where all the power lies. It rescued me all those years ago and would do so again.

Staying motivated when things don't seem to be coming together is a challenge at times. How do you motivate yourself? What would you advise someone else?

"A BRAIN IS A TERRIBLE THING TO WASTE."

Days start with my brain running. That can take me down a lane I rather my day not include, so I know I am not afforded the luxury of lingering in my bed. Most mornings, fill my eyes with spectacular snapshots of the day's sunrise. None are ever the same. The moment arrives to toss the covers aside, springing to go and meet with God. In "my chair", in "that room". I find a cup of coffee in my hands and I just sit. Being still. Waiting. The day's scripture settles my mind opening my heart to gratitude. Again.

"FAITH SPEED BUMPS"

The eighteen weeks of chemotherapy are my great spiritual training ground for what has occurred since and lending understanding to what transpired before. Nothing confronts me with my true self like suffering. Ouch. Time to take inventory. How is my gratitude? What does God think? What would my BFF say in truth and love? Motivation comes from our Father. This truth removes all that pressure we like to place on ourselves. Why would we do that, forgetting that we had been bought and paid for at such a HIGH price? What's left? Gratitude and Love.

TRUST AND OBEY.

"I prayed to the Lord and He answered me. He freed me from ALL my fears....Oh, the JOYS of those who take refuge in Him", (Psalm 34: 4, 8; emphasis mine).

God is good. He gives me all I NEED for a preserving will to obey during any crisis when my feelings become "great masqueraders of authority." I become less able to see God clearly.

He can: deliver, sustain, strengthen, comfort, heal, save and provide. My distress, if embraced, is where God loves to show up! He desires me to experience who He is, allowing the measures necessary to achieve it. "He leads me in the paths of righteousness for His name's sake…" (Psalm 23: 3b). I had felt "stripped" of everything I imagined my life would look like before 50. When I chose to obey, God responded-sometimes in amazing ways, in others with the simple but priceless presence of His peace. FIRST OBEDIENCE, then His power operating within and through me, experiencing His best.

It isn't that easy.

But it is that simple.

So, here's the COMMUNICATION part.

My first three rounds of chemotherapy went smoothly: chemo on Friday, down and out until Monday, back to life by Tuesday with burnt taste buds, loose nails, hair loss and eyes tearing 24/7. Round 4 and 5 blindsided me with HELL WEEK. I had never experienced such darkness and despair. I had hoped that round 4 was just a fluke. When it returned at round 5, "knocking me back to YESTERDAY", I was at a complete loss. I ran into a seasoned survivor at church and her advice? Tell my friends. As I did, reaffirming the depth of darkness, they asked why I had not called or reached out. You would probably offer your explanation and move on. I had to deal with a heart matter that was confronted during these "teachable moments" from God. I had to make a choice to do things "my way" or "God's way." I do know that "God's way is ALWAYS right." God gives you moments to consider a decision. Use it and you won't find yourself dealing with the same heart matter in the future. To remain hurt that my friends weren't around during those two rounds of chemotherapy would allow the enemy a foothold in my heart.

Choosing to be vulnerable, I opened up, sharing about the battle being waged over my soul. Astonished that I had not called my friends, it simply NEVER occurred to me. My mind was darkened by the cumulative effects of the same drugs we hoped would save me.

God planned my final 6th round just after Thanksgiving, saving His best for last: Gratitude + Humility + Communication = Joy of my Salvation.

Habakkuk 3:17-19 reads,
"Even though...;
Even though...;
Even though...,
Yet I will rejoice in the Lord!
I will be joyful in the God of my salvation!
He makes me as surefooted as a deer,
able to tread upon the heights".

In your opinion, what does it really take to win live at dealing with life challenges?

REMEMBER.

Remembering Jesus throughout my day, who He is, and what He has done in my life. With a pen and paper, list ALL He has done for you, your family, and friends. Look at your Face Book, Pinterest or scrap book. What do you see?

Have you sat outside lately?
The warmth of the sun wraps itself around you.
God whispers your name in the wind.

The grass waves to you with the animals of the field going about their day.

Moving to an equestrian community seventeen years ago, our daughter with Autism participated in activities that were beyond therapeutic. Our personal adventure began three years ago when we adopted three female Pygmy goats. They are veteran mothers much to everyone's delight. Their babies frolicking with one another is my afternoon matinee. They climb, sometimes each other and hop, skip, flop and magically spring forward in a front summersault landing with a half twist! I'm witnessing pure unadulterated FUN by creatures who know how to live without a care.

REMEMBER.

Who do you belong to? Whose precious daughter? Who created your inmost being? Who knows all the days ordained for you, before they came to be? Who knows and cares for your anxious thoughts? Who is waiting to bless you with the peace that surpasses ALL understanding? Who has taken you by your right hand? Who is sheltering you under His wing? Who? It's our Heavenly Father, who graciously gives us every good and perfect gift without finding fault.

REMEMBER.
"...And BE THANKFUL. "(Colossians 3:12-15, emphasis mine).

Peter offers a great plan in 2Peter 1:5-8:
"For this very reason, make every effort to add to your faith goodness;
and to goodness, knowledge;
and to knowledge, self-control;
and to self-control, perseverance;

and to perseverance, godliness;
and to godliness, mutual affection;
and to mutual affection, love.

For if you possess these qualities in increasing measure, they will keep you from being ineffective and unproductive in your knowledge of our Lord Jesus Christ."

Every detail for living productively is addressed. A pitfall awaits when OUR plans run askew. Stay tuned.

One of the biggest struggles people have is feeling like they are a failure or dealing with failure in general. What are your views on the topic of dealing with failure?

FAILURE IS NOT AN OPTION.

This defines my generation. How does a sheltered minority woman cope, overcome and/or reach that fruitless standard? It's an open invitation to pride which God promises to oppose. When Psalms (Psalm 73) describes pride as a necklace it is because we can't see it, but you can bet that everyone else does!

Define Failure. Or, do you let others define Failure?

Maturity should push us past the fallacy that achieving the "American Dream" is tied to the paradigm of "keeping up with the Jones." What is worse than comparing yourself to others is comparing yourself to who you thought you were before your world became unrecognizable. *"Our ways are not God's ways"*...and neither are our thoughts (Isaiah 55:8-9). The cross must finish its work through every crevice in our hearts. Are you discouraged? Perhaps your expectations jumped track from God's will for your life? The tighter we hold onto our dreams, the more painful it is for God to pry them loose one finger at a time. Remember too that *"The thief comes only to steal and kill and destroy; I have come that they may have life, and have it to the full"* (John 10:10). This fullness grows on both sides of the fence: life's greatest lows and its highs. Alter your expectations while awaiting God to reveal His plan in His time. Amazing things will happen. This is not your kingdom. It is His and His alone. Let yours go.

PERSEVERANCE

Our lives are not only journeys in the softer sense but a marathon of endurance and perseverance. Your faith is proved genuine through trials and *"we consider blessed those who have persevered"* (James 5:11). I can feel that I am being asked to "Grin and Bear it!" But do we really have a choice? Not one that I could negotiate in the condition I was in. God had my FULL attention confronting me on another heart matter: SHALOM.

He himself is our peace (Ephesians 2:16). I thought peace was a gift. The TRUTH: He is to be my peace. Your peace. *"He has come into our hearts...to establish His reign. And, His reign is where all blessings abound. That's where we are to live: in the place of blessing."* This is my heart's new home. One breath at a time. I count my blessings again because therein lies my HOPE. *"Victory is not won by strength but by perseverance-where God does His handiwork."* I made peace with letting go of my plans and dreams.

GOD IS IN THE DETAILS: PRAYER

If God is in the details, praying will follow suit.

"When I consider your heavens,
the work of your fingers,
the moon and the stars,
which you have set in place,
what is man (Yolanda) that you are mindful of him (Me),
the son of man that you care for him (Me)?"
(Psalm 8: 3, 4; emphasis mine).

Prayers come while sitting in the stillness of the morning. Waiting. Waiting for God. You'll hear what He's asking of you when you obey his command to "Be Still."

On one of my recent visual pasture checks, I saw two of the triplets on one side of the back pasture and the third playing separately with Fat Tuesday, Mistletoe's first born. Returning from one of my errands I noticed a gaggle of vultures roosting in one of our trees while several more circled the sky. My heart sank. I had one more errand to run and as I left, I watched to see if any were making light on anything on the ground. They were holding the same pattern on my return. I also saw that the triplet's mother, Betty had not moved in the time I was away. I changed into my muck shoes and pasture shirt. Running through the garage, I grabbed the horse crop affording me confidence I would not get kicked if the horses began one of their pecking order exercises. I realized Betty, had foolishly pushed her head through the fencing and her beautiful crown of thorns thwarted her attempts to pull free.
OH.
MY.
My mind raced: How long have you been here?
Long enough for the vultures to smell blood.
What thoughts have you given to your babies?
Do you think about those kind of things?

I bet you won't do this again…!

GET THERE QUICKER!

Her head was high enough in the fencing that any possibility of sitting or lying down to rest had not been an option. Approaching her made her yammering even louder as she squirmed with all the strength and fight left in her body. I grabbed the hair on the back of her neck and her horns with my other hand. The first pass unsuccessful, I tightened my grasp of hair just enough that the yammering stopped. It's hard to scream when you can't breathe. After the second try, she was off running as fast as those short legs could muster and "The Mother and Child Reunion" song was playing in my head (LOL).

"The Lord will fight for you; you need only to be still." (Exodus 14:14).

As life has happened, His blessings are personal victories. Some BLOW. MY. MIND. Some are treasures in my heart. ALL are kisses from God. Decide that the enemy will NOT trip you with his "failure mindset." He thrives in sending us into a downward spiral spiritually, mentally and emotionally. Any victory, no matter how small, is still a victory. Let gratitude bathe you, while realizing how often you have sidestepped that mine field. Invite God to fill the holes in your heart with Himself. He's your roadside assistance and He's better than AAA. His warranty is eternal.

"…God is the strength of my heart and my portion forever."
(Psalm 73:26)

What advice would you give to someone who is ready to reclaim and live their sparkle?

ARE YOU READY FOR THIS?

Our motivation to change occurs once the pain of the status quo overrides our fear(s).

WRONG WAY, RIGHT WAY.

Recently during a family dinner, our adult son spoke to us about the expectations of others and the role they can play in our thinking and in our lives from one decision to another. As a young couple in a dynamic church we had been encouraged to participate in the leadership and to dream about how God could use us to His Glory. I immaturely made that a topic of many marital conversations asking Jim about his dreams. Nothing. Nada. I couldn't have any of that, especially sporting that big 'ol pride necklace in my marriage. A few rounds of vulnerable conversations later, my friends informed me that Jim did have a dream. Great! Please clue me in! Jim's dream: to see his family to heaven. That is why he is my soulmate. God gives us what we need and He knew I needed my Jim. My heart loves him more, when while spilling out my poorly motivated frustration, he broke into such laughter that reminded me how much we've grown in our marriage and how much God has preserved it through trials suffered by my ambition and pride. WRONG WAY.

What leads you in your decision making? Or, who leads you? During my first 25 years of life, there was a plan. There's comfort in a plan. It offers a false sense of control. There was high school, followed by college and thank you God, medical school. Your residency placement offers you a place in the field of your choice. I could say my career was hijacked but my decision to step out of medicine during my final year of pediatric residency was divinely designed. Our return to Texas with our 3-year-old daughter and 6-month old son proved a brutal transition with both children contracting chicken pox. Jaxson was hospitalized for dehydration despite our medical training. He would sip a bit then nap at most, fifteen minutes. Sometimes when a patient is admitted, it addresses both the patient's and caregiver's needs. I was on my knees in delirium.

Each of these "faith speed bumps", including the loss of our unborn child, Zöe Marie, has a recurring lesson. When you hit an unexpected bump while driving, everything that is not secured properly immediately takes flight. Suspended in animation, is much how I feel in those life moments. God uses that space to develop my spiritual muscles where only prayer will move my heart from worry and despair...to Faith.

"Even though I walk through the valley of the shadow of death, I will fear no evil, For YOU. ARE. WITH. ME;" (Psalm 23:4, emphasis mine). RIGHT WAY <3.

Examine the motivation of your heart. The above experiences were consumed with great heartache, but each found me in communion with God, eventually. I shared the depth of my heart break, asking for both spiritual and practical advice. The breakthroughs came throwing myself down before God begging for His will to become mine; to create in me a new heart; and, to forgive me of my lack of faith by not trusting His hand. It is beyond reason we could think we have the slightest bit of control in our lives. My advice? Never let go of the Hand that is guiding you.

RIGHT WAY. BE TEACHABLE.

Especially in your most vulnerable of circumstances. We had moved to a smaller town for the school district. Those first three years were years of lament. Crying. You know, the UGLY CRY. One day I was so loud my black lab matched me with his own version of a bark and howl sonata. I decided I wasn't going to do that again and then laughed. Here's the thing. If you allow your decisions to be rooted in faith and moved along by obedience and love, the AMAZING happens. Fast forward nine years and be the fly on the wall of Rey's graduation celebration. We celebrated the irreplaceable roles The Village played behind a beautiful, productive and one the happiest of souls most will ever meet. We are periodically reminded of the impact she has on family, friends and strangers in every area of her life. Can parents possibly ask for more? The DFW Center for Autism has since replicated itself statewide, merged with a national organization funded by government grants and offers families the same hope of our dreams.

"You anoint my head with oil; my cup overflows." (Psalm 23:5b)
RIGHT WAY.

"… No eye has seen
No ear has heard
And
No mind has imagined
What GOD has prepared
For those who love HIM." (1 Corinthians 2:9, emphasis mine).

A work in progress. It's the constant state of my heart and soul. These days it just happens to have caution tape around it. We are on Holy ground and the fight over our souls is real on days of bountiful blessings and overwhelming trials. Life is not about my plan. It is about my path. Your path is one decision at a time in the love powered by your relationship with God. That realization takes all the pressure off. Your life becomes a matter of choosing trust vs fear, peace vs anxiety, joy vs discouragement and then sprinkle that with smart vs stupid. God's rainbows in your life will arc from Faith + Obedience to Blessing + Hope, ushering you into the love story He has written for you. Blessings + Hope provides endurance. And perseverance. To His Glory.

"Surely your goodness and love
will follow me
all the days of my life,
…" (Psalm 23:6).

What "must have" resources would you recommend someone use daily in keeping focused, motivated, and encouraged?

"Therefore do not throw away your confidence,
which has a great reward.
For you have need of endurance, …" (Hebrews 10:35, 36).

Know that God gives all I need.

YOLANDA'S TOP TEN:

#10…BOOKS
God has used people who are more adept at characterizing His nature with their pen. A commentary on the book of Isaiah or an in-depth study on the life of David, served me well in my practice of repentance.

#9...TIME

I take this for granted. It is just a mist and therefore important that it is used well. "...the thankful heart will find, in every hour, some heavenly blessings." –Henry Ward Beecher

#8...PEOPLE

It's strange to place people below the other seven. God uses people to do sooo much: to usher in His Kingdom; to teach, rebuke and admonish; to epitomize His nature through obedience and love (Agape Love) for one another. In David's hours of need, God used David's family, the band of mighty men and a prophet. It is number 8 because of my tendency to idolize what people think of me vs my personal relationship with God, my first resort for strength through prayer.

#7...NATURE'S ELEMENTS: RAIN

My mom says rain are God's tears from Heaven. Life is not without shedding tears in joy or sorrow. My heart cannot forget my sin's responsibility for the Death of Jesus.

#6...WIND

A gentle wind whispers my name through the trees outside "my room" in "my chair". Texas has Tornado Alley. Its greatest work of beauty lies in the Grand Canyon.

#5...SUN

The sun is a double-edged sword. The sun makes an unmistakable impression. Closing my eyes and lifting my head, I feel its warmth invading every pore of my being, waking me up to its power. Witnessing a Texas Sunrise and Sunset is nothing short of a miracle. They leave their brilliant canvas of colors etched in my mind.

#4...MUSIC

Melodies surround my heart, lifting it through a song's verse, its chorus. A week prior to my operation, I videoed songs of worship. God allows my heart to soar in worship. During my days of chemotherapy, He greeted me each morning with a love song in my head, already playing in my waking moments. God is Good All the Time.

#3...THE 5 SENSES: Sight, Hearing, Touch, Smell, Taste

A friend has three of her four sons are affected with autism. Like me, she has a background in medicine as a Care Flight nurse. She worked the devastating 1985 Delta crash at DFW. She has great insight in how our environment is perceived by those affected with autism. Setting up a room with five different radios at full blast, she had everyone put on a pair of dizzying eye lenses, clothes of various weights and textures...well you get the idea. Their senses are constantly overwhelmed. Blood work confirms this with elevated levels of stress hormones. My point is, we have these senses to help us develop a "sense" of what our Father is like. We are created in His image, but these come with a warning: the truth that there can be "Too Much of a Good Thing." Carry on.

#2...MY NATURE

My sinful nature. It will always serve to remind me of my need for God. He has also blessed us with gifts. Our femininity allows our emotions, properly channeled, to glorify Him. I am drawn to compassion, empathy, hope and their works. Their alter egos are indifference, pride and fear which register in my lifetime to a fault. Choose to submit to His path. Your life résumé will be what you cannot imagine!

#1…HIS WORD

"For the word of God is living and active…it judges the thoughts and attitudes of the heart". (Hebrews 4:12)

His word will always be relevant.

"…The LORD'S word is flawless;
He shields all who take refuge in him." (Psalm18:30)

Please share 5 of your favorites scriptures, quotes or poems that you have referenced when you needed encouragement.

For those who would learn God's ways, humility if the first thing, humility is the second, humility is the third.
- Augustine

Before we can pray "Thy Kingdom come," we must be willing to pray, "My kingdom go."
- Alan Redpath

Always Pray (Ephesians 6:18): Communication is critical in a time of war…This is where the battle is truly fought-on our knees."
-Chris Tiegreen

The Road to Wholeness (Isaiah 42:6): "Never let go of the hand that leads you."
 -Chris Tiegreen

*Hope Against Hope (Romans 4:18): Our faith wages epic battles against our sight, and we must always let faith win."
-Chris Tiegreen

What makes you a woman that is an overcomer?

What is my TRUTH?
"For everyone born of God overcomes the world…" (1John 5:4)

"If you say, 'The Lord is my refuge,' … he will command his angels concerning you to guard you in all your ways;" (Psalm 91:9-11).

"I keep my eyes always on the LORD. With him at my right hand, I cannot be shaken." (Psalm 16:8)

YOLANDA CONTRERAS TAYLOR

 Yolanda Contreras Taylor is known among her friends and family as a fighter. Born in 1962 in the Dallas area, Yolanda matured into a high achiever, getting her undergraduate degree from Texas A&M and later her medical degree from the University of Texas in San Antonio. Early in her medical career she gave birth to her daughter, Reyna, who doctors later diagnosed with autism. Yolanda quit her medical residency to provide the care her young daughter needed. Yolanda went on to have a son, Jaxson, and after Jaxson a late term miscarriage. During all this, Yolanda and her husband, Jim still co-founded the DFW Center for Autism and spearheaded immunization efforts with the Dallas Area Infant Immunization Coalition for at-risk children in the Dallas Metro area. Yolanda has battled fibromyalgia, breast cancer, and depression. She has met each challenge with the same grit and determination that define her as a person.

Email: Lalazmd88@gmail.com
Facebook: https://www.facebook.com/Lalazmd

AMANDA COOPER

What one word would you use to describe yourself and why did you choose that word?

Enterprising: Marked by an independent energetic spirit and by readiness to act. I chose this word for its uniqueness. As the oldest of four daughters I have always been fiercely independent and wanted to be my own boss, always looking for my own path, determined at tackling obstacles and finding solutions. For whatever reason, I have always gone against the grain or norm, and never had a fear of having a difference of opinion or having an "enterprising" attitude.

Share with us about an experience you faced that challenged you and placed you in a situation where you had to make tough decisions? How did you overcome it?

One incident that provides great insight into how I became who I was is one that I have not shared with many. I grew up in a very Christian home, my parents pastored most my life and I felt like I lived in church, I had very high standards and moral expectations to live up to. At 15 I was very involved in my youth group and can honestly say I was a really good kid, the year before I had even traveled to Australia to minister for two weeks. In late fall of this year our church held a huge rally and thousands of people came from all over the country for a weekend of worship, camping and fellowship. I and several of my girlfriends had talked our parents into letting us camp out just like hundreds of others did on the grounds. I could hardly wait to spend time with my friends, it was going to be the most fabulous fun time ever!

What happened this weekend turned out to be the most horrific and haunting instances of my life. There are very few things teenage girls think about more than.... you guessed it, BOYS. In my case, there was this one particular boy, you know him well. This is the boy all the girls thought was cute, he was a celebrity of sorts because his Dad was a very well-known evangelist he was older, tall, built, and cool, and knew just how to smile and make your heart beat 1000 beats per second.

Well, this boy was at the rally this weekend from out of state and my friends and I ran into him within an hour of the first evening. For story sake let's call this boy Mike. Mike came with a friend and they were more than happy to invite my friends and I to hang out later and selected a meeting place in one of the fields nearby. Just a little back story in good ole Texas field parties, hangouts were popular, bales of hay and beautiful stars were the backdrop. At I'm guessing around 8 or 9 we met up with the boys and they had beer. Most of us girls had never tasted beer and if we had it was a sip or two. We hung out a while and Mike was really acting like he was into me, I couldn't believe it. I didn't even think he knew my name in the few years I had known him. He was really focused on me and giving me undivided attention.

It started getting later and my girlfriend's thought we should head back. Mike suggested I stay a little longer and his car was not far, he would drive me back to the tent in a bit. Not wanting to disappoint the older cooler guy who I had had a crush on for what felt like a lifetime, I happily agreed even though my gut was telling me to leave with my friends. They, in total jealousy agreed to let me stay and they made their way back to the tent area. As soon as they left Mike got closer, he held my hand and began to kiss me. I didn't even really know how to kiss nor did I want to, I was shy but I didn't want to seem uncool.

At that point, I decided to chug a beer, my nerves were all over the place and after about 10 minutes my skinny frame was buzzed. Apparently, it was evident because Mike started trying to touch me and I voiced feeling uncomfortable, but it wasn't appreciated, in fact it made him mad. Mike asked why I stayed if I was going to be lame and I said I was leaving, but I didn't get that chance. Mike called his friend over and they pushed and forced me to the cold hard grassy ground. Mikes' friend got on his knees above my head and held my arms and wrists extended straight out while Mike held my legs from moving with his knees and hands. For what felt like hours I was brutally raped multiple times by them. That night I lost my virginity, I lost my innocence and was damaged goods. I was physically sick, bruised and bloody and every part of my body hurt and from that moment on I lost respect for men and myself. For almost 15 years I held this story in because after all it was my fault it happened, so I thought.

In 2001, at 21 I married my high school sweetheart, I was determined to have the "perfect" life I was made to think was ideal. By 28, I had two gorgeous daughters Avery, 4 and Amelia, 1. I lived a seemingly fabulous life, impeccable home, loving husband, beautiful kids, as a stay at home Mom I was living the dream, timeshares, social groups, material things, etc. except I wasn't happy. During this time of unhappiness, I began having an affair and it opened the door for me to see things very unclearly, as if everything was wrong in my life, except me. It was exciting, I felt beautiful and sexy, I felt appreciated and valued, and I felt loved. The only problem was that the problem wasn't my marriage, it was me, I wasn't living the life that I wanted, I was living the life I thought I was supposed to want.

In the process, I hurt a lot of people, destroyed my family, and I uprooted my children from all stability. By 29, I was divorced, jobless, homeless, and basically wanted nothing to do with anything that had to do with family. I was tired of being a Mom, I was tired of being a wife, and I was tired of living a life that I chose but didn't know why or want anymore. I gave up, and I was living in a very selfish, very fast and very destructive pattern. In keeping up with my lifestyle I thought I deserved I resorted to compromising my values and dignity so that I could be "happy", I changed out men like underwear, I wanted nothing to do with love or commitment. I got physically involved with a married man who was a real estate mogul, it was perfect I didn't have to intimately commit or share emotions and I got everything I needed monetarily.

One weekend while in Vegas he made a deal with me to give me money to start a business, $600,000 later I became the sole owner of a night club. I was living a dream that most people would give a limb to have and I was living large. About a year and a half into my "new life" on a Sunday morning after a night out partying, I woke up feeling like death and sobbed for about 3 hours straight on my bathroom floor. My life wasn't better, I wasn't happier, my life was worse than ever, I was living a life surrounded by insane amounts of sin, I had no relationship with my daughters or God and I was utterly miserable, I know now that was the first of the calls the Holy Spirit had to make to get me out of my selfish coma.

The road back was a tough one. There were days that my kids and I went without electricity, that I would have them helping me search the house for coins so that I could put gas in my car to get them to school and me to work, I was rarely ever able to buy groceries over the amount of $100 a month. We were living in the miracle zone and I had to stretch my money so far it still is beyond me, like Jesus feeding 5000 with 5 loaves of bread and two fish. I was determined to do things the right way and I was going to do it all on my own. I was going to make up for all the mistakes I made and I was going to prove to everyone I was worthy of them loving me again.

One strong attribute I have is work ethic, I can honestly say I don't know many people that can hold a candle to what I can get done if focused. That started paying off and I got several promotions at work and things were looking up, my girls and I were starting a new life together. It was during this time that I realized I needed help, I needed to know why I couldn't get close to people, why I had commitment issues, why I wasn't happy, why I hurt people?

After almost three years of counseling the answer was not what I expected, the untreated rape incident that had happened over 15 years before had caused irreparable damage. In very vague terms my counselor broke it down, I couldn't intimately love others, my children, my husband, my family, my friends, because I didn't love myself, subconsciously I didn't think I was worthy of love. How in the heck could that be? I had a new inflated sense of ego, I was pretty, I was fit, I was smart, I was making my own money, I was dating very successful men, I was traveling, I was envied. But I was empty space, I was living a, superficial life and offered nothing to anyone and served zero purpose.

During this time, I became a very highly functioning drinker. As most of you know drinking in excess in any fashion does not lead to good things, and yep you guessed it I started repeating all the same patterns, infidelity, selfishness, and I hid all of this very well. Once again from the outside everything looked perfect, but it was all a lie. During this 5 year stint, I fell in love and started dating my now boyfriend, and it was a mess with a capital M. The relationship was so highly dysfunctional that it almost became a drug in its self, we were both messed up, both hurting each other both selfish, both having affairs, both not showing our children any kind of normalcy, one of us at any given time was one foot in and one foot out at any time.

I am mentioning this because out of this ridiculous relationship I found out how to love myself and how to really love someone else.

It started with forgiveness, not of others but of myself. How could anyone ever love someone as ugly as me on the inside, this monster I had become, who cares what I looked like on the outside, I was diseased on the inside. How did I want to be remembered? What legacy am I leaving if the people closest to me didn't even know the real me? I wanted to change, and so I did, just like that and I have changed. I took baby steps, worked on repairing the relationships with those I hurt, by apologizing, by showing up when they needed me, not because it was what I wanted to do, but because it was what I was called to do.

I started praying for God to give me the desire to love my children and want to be their mom. I prayed for God to allow me to forgive the deep hurts that others had caused me. I believed that I was forgiven and made new and I was, since then I let it go. I rarely think about that person I became and when I do I love her and can now laugh about it, that poor old Amanda was hurting, was trying to figure it out and by the grace of God she made it out to tell her story. This story is far from over and do I mess up. DAILY! I am the first to say that I screw up all the time, but when I do I pick myself up, dust off the dirt and I start over.

I've learned that if I have to do that every day until the moment I take last my breath that it's ok. I live in a constant state of forgiveness, acceptance and grace. Those who know me can tell you that I could be loving them one moment and biting their head off the next, I'm high strung, I'm demanding and I am a self-proclaimed control freak, but I am also a giver and loyal to the core. If you are a valued person in my life, intimately, in friendship, or even in business I would run through nails to protect you and make sure that you know that you matter. A colleague of mine said a phrase to me once and it stuck, "If you get to the end of your life and you can say "Well, that didn't suck", then you did pretty well."

Staying motivated when things don't seem to be coming together is a challenge at times. How do you motivate yourself? What advice would you give someone else?

I have this weird big imaginary restart button in my brain, kind of the like the one on the "Family Feud "show. When I am feeling stuck, or defeated I take that challenge or problem and take control of it by pressing the restart button and asking myself what I need to do, to change my actions or reactions to get a different outcome. One thing I learned in the many years of counseling is to use positive imagery. In my case I stop, clear my mind and thoughts in that very moment and I focus on MY happy place, for me it's skiing down a mountain. I take in the sun beating down, warming me, the way the clear air feels on my face and the sounds of nature and snow being cut by my ski's. In that moment, I am in control and am creating the path I choose and what direction I want to go. I use that as a metaphor for the current obstacle I am experiencing and I face the challenge head on.

In your opinion, what does it really take to win at dealing with life challenges?

Grace. Having grace for yourself and for others is the most important virtue we can have in life. Unfortunately, we are NOT perfect, contrary to the popular majority's belief. Ha-ha! I screw up probably 100 times a day and people are going to fail me 100 times a day, it's a part of being real. The definition of grace is this: The influence of spirit of God operating in humans to regenerate or strengthen them. How cool is that? I don't know about you but I sure as heck can use regeneration and strength and I know that the people in my life deserve that as well.

One of the biggest struggles people have is feeling like they are a failure or dealing with failure in general. What are your views on the topic of dealing with failure?

Failure and fear of rejection are probably the two things I have struggled with most in my life. I tend to be a perfectionist in every area of my life, if I am not succeeding or being "the best" at something - I am failing. It's never in fear of someone else's opinion but only to the high expectations I have for myself. One thing I remind myself of when I get to a place when I feel like I need a big "L" on my forehead is to look back at some of the most successful people who were once considered total failures. Walt Disney's first animation company went bankrupt, he was also turned down 302 times before he got financing for creating Disney World. Albert Einstein didn't speak until 4 and didn't read until 7. If those guys can do it why the heck can't I? What do they have that I don't? Absolutely nothing!

What advice would you give to someone who is ready to reclaim and live their sparkle?

Be Authentic!!!!! There is only one you, and you are perfect just as you are. Can we be better? Yes, but you are a far better bonafide, genuine, certified one and only you, than a copycat of someone you think you should be. One other thing I think is important is to feel qualified. It's easy to look at our own lives and all the crap that's wrong with it, whether it's current or past mistakes, secrets and demons and think who am I to give advice or be "qualified" to help others. Guess what? That is what makes you the MOST qualified, turn your junk from past and present into your purpose.

What "must have" resources would you recommend someone use daily in keeping focused, motivated and encouraged?

I am a singer and a HUGE music person, my must haves for productivity and best focus occurs when I have music. Sometimes this music is quiet, sometimes at alarming decibels, sometimes its praise and worship, sometimes its gangsta rap….

Please share 5 of your favorite scriptures, quotes or poem's that you have referenced when you needed encouragement.

Okay, so I am a very systematic person, almost to a superstitious level, like a ball player wearing the same dirty socks for every game in a winning streak. Every morning I am by myself whether dropping kids at school, headed to a meeting or office, my day is not complete until I blare "Diva" by Beyoncé. I think everyone should have a theme song, pick one that relates or motivates you and claim it as yours. In the signature line of my email I have my favorite quote by Beverly Sills, "There are no shortcuts to anyplace worth going", I love Proverbs 31:20, "She opens her arms to the poor and extends her hands to the needy" we should NEVER be too good to help others that can't do anything for us. I also love this African Proverb "When the roots are deep, there is no reason to fear the wind." Picture the wind as the, the abusive husband, the difficult boss, the addiction, the anxiety or eating disorder, that nagging obstacle that we have the power to control. Lastly, "Your smile is your logo, your personality is your business card, how you leave others feeling after they have an experience with you becomes your trademark." By Jay Danzie.

What makes you a woman that is an overcomer?

I am an overcomer because I am authentic, I am not ashamed of my mistakes and scars and I wear them as a badge of courage and a testimony to others that it's ok to make mistakes. I am an overcomer because I am beautiful, I do not have imperfections, I have uniqueness and I have gotten good at being me. I am an overcomer because I am worthy of giving and receiving love not based off my performance or how others perform for me, but because I, we are all just a moment away from our next failure but also from the next VICTORY!

AMANDA COOPER

Amanda is a native Fort Worth girl and rarely meets a stranger in this town. As the oldest of four daughters, it was fitting she became an Alpha Female at a young age. Prior to the mortgage industry she worked in Hotel and Golf Course Interior Design and in Commercial and Multifamily Property Management, it was here that she found her passion in working with people. In 2013 Amanda became a licensed loan officer, known now as "The Mortgage Chick".

Amanda resides in Colleyville, Texas with her family and is involved in many philanthropic groups and leadership committees. Amanda loves to travel, and has extensively but by far her favorite place is Dubai. For fun, she enjoys cooking, skiing, gardening and family movie nights.

Phone: 817-689-2987
Email: Amanda.Cooper@SenteMortgage.com
Website: www.AmandaCooperMortgage.com

TINA LAREA

What one word would you use to describe yourself and why did you choose that word?

LOVE – My primary life pursuit is to show up and love (#ShowUpAndLove). Love is the principle upon which all other Godly principles hang. God is love, and when we love as He loves, we are demonstrating the most powerfully complex and virtuous action that we can possibly demonstrate: we are sharing God. Love sets the captive free; love unbinds the one who is bound; love transforms. Love never fails. Where Godly love abounds, grace, mercy, compassion, wisdom, and authority also abide.

From childhood, I've known conceptually that God loves me and that He forgave me before I ever missed a mark. But *knowing* the love of God came for me personally when I realized that I am loved without an agenda, with absolutely no expectation. When I could just be honest about everything in my life with absolutely no judgment, no condemnation, no expectation, I felt free! I could trust openly and allow myself to bring into the light everything for which I felt ashamed. Once I brought everything into the light, and there was no condemnation toward me, I was able to grow. Much like a seed will grow much better in a nutrient rich soil, so was I in my new "love-without-agenda" environment. Love set me free! Therefore, I pursue love and to love others this way. I am called to set the captive free. Love is the way.

One day I had a vision. I was walking along a road with Jesus. He was to my left, I was to His right. We were both walking with our hands behind our backs, just talking as we went along. But then He stopped walking and He nodded to the right as if to point out something to me. I looked to my right and saw a person sitting on the sidewalk and leaning somewhat against the wall of a building. The person's head was downward, resting on their knees so that the face was not revealed. I could not determine if the person was man or woman. Jesus asked me, "Do you see that one over there?" "Yes, Lord. I see," I replied. He said, "Tina, if I told you that I gave you the authority to set the captive free, would you do that for me?" "Yes, Lord, of course I would!" And He told me, "Go set them free." So, I walked over to the one sitting on the sidewalk and unbound the hands of the one who was bound and returned to Jesus. He said to me, "This is the call on your life. Go set the captives free."

Share with us about an experience you faced that challenged you and placed you in a situation where you had to make tough decisions? How did you overcome it?

I was desperate. I wouldn't be able to endure this day or the days that followed without God's complete intervention. So, I sought Him, and He spoke. He told me, "When you see the great cloud of witnesses, the vast army that will be against you, do not fear or be dismayed, for I am the Lord your God, and I have come to deliver victory to you today." I was reading from the Bible, but He was speaking directly to me. I had no idea what He was practically talking about, but I took His encouraging word and held on tightly to it. I got dressed, kissed my children as they went off to school, and then I left for the day's agenda.

When I arrived at my destination, I went inside and was standing in the hallway of this public facility when God spoke, "Tina, do you love me?" "Yes, LORD, I love you." Once again, "Tina, do you love me?" Once again, I said, "Yes, LORD, you know that I love you." Then He asked, "Do you trust me?" I replied, "I trust You." He said to me, "Do you remember that you told me that you wanted to be accounted as righteous just as Abraham was accounted as righteous?" "Yes, I remember," I replied. Then He said, "If you want to be accounted as righteous just as Abraham, then you must have the faith of Abraham. Abraham's faith is what accounted him as righteous. I required of Abraham to give up his son, to lay him down, a sacrifice. I required the same of myself when I laid down my son, a sacrifice. And now I'm requiring it of you. You must choose this day in whom you will trust, whom you will love, above and before all things in heaven and in the earth."

I had a decision to make. I cried and told God that this is a hard thing, an incomprehensible requirement to ask of a momma who loves her children more than anything to lay them down. But God remembered what I had forgotten. I had asked God for righteousness, to love HIM above and before ALL things, not knowing at the time of my request that my children would be considered in my decision. This meant that I would have to completely trust Him with His plan for their lives and mine. Now it was decision time. So, I stood up, right there in the hallway; I turned my body around, looked up and lifted my palms up and said, "I turn my face like a flint toward you. I love you and I trust you." Just like that, in that moment, I laid down everything in my life, right into the hands of my God, a sacrifice. My all. It wasn't the first time I was faced with choosing God first, and it wouldn't be the last.

Staying motivated when things don't seem to be coming together is a challenge at times. How do you motivate yourself? What would you advise someone else?

Boy, have God and I had some tay-to-tays over this one! I've literally locked myself in a bedroom for days, writhing around in spiritual and emotional pain, opening my Bible and pointing to Scripture and asking God, "Why doesn't my life look like this promise right here?" as if God had been called onto the carpet to answer me. After days of wrestling like this, I finally submitted that whatever I was going through was for my good because God loves me and His ways are higher than my ways and His plan never fails. Basically, I had to come to the end of myself and trust Him.

One such time occurred when I was living in Texas. My husband and I had worked diligently for years to launch our company, but to no avail. We finally decided that, after all the failures, we would just give it up and become full time ministers. I remember it like it was yesterday. We stood in the kitchen and said, "We're done. Let's just let it all go and teach people about Jesus." We would be giving up everything in our lives and my husband's lifelong dream to own his own company. The company was too expensive in every way to hang onto, so we made the decision to lay it all down and move forward into full time ministry.

That night, we both had the same dream; and in that dream, the Lord told us that we were off the path and in a ditch and we needed to get back up onto the road that He had prepared for us. We felt like we were on a roller coaster. Nevertheless, we obeyed and made the choice to stick with the plan to launch the company. We knew that only God could make it happen though, so we were going to have to trust Him and just take one day at a time, following His lead and allowing His plan to unfold. That's what we chose then and what we continue to choose daily.

Each one of us is given a platform from which God's voice can speak if we will let Him, if we will coordinate with Him, work with Him, and not try to man-handle our lives. God is never early or late. His plan is always on time. In challenging times, I eventually choose to trust Him, although it's not always easy. I would also add that the fervent prayers of family and friends are instrumental in my motivation. Without them, I don't know how I would have survived. There is no repaying such a priceless gift; but I can pray for them as well and continue to show up and love in their lives. My motivation is God's faithfulness and the prayers prayed on my behalf. I would recommend that everyone get some praying people behind them for support and to also be the praying person for others, and to trust that God has you and your future in the palm of His hands.

In your opinion, what does it really take to win at dealing with life's challenges?

Three things: understanding where life's challenges originated, what to do about that, and then trusting God.

Life's challenges began in the Garden of Eden where iniquity was birthed and is passed down from one generation to the next. Iniquity is twisted thinking, or thinking in a way that conflicts with God's thinking. Iniquity is an internal conflict that presents itself externally in many forms: abandonment, abuse, addictions, anger, anxiety, being judgmental, blaming, co-dependency, complaining, compromise, control, cowardice, criticism, deceitfulness, deception, defensiveness, defiance, depression, doubt, drama, envy, fear, focusing on the past, guilt, hate, hopelessness, illness, insecurity, jealousy, judging, lack of purpose, living in the past, needing to please others, negativity, poor self-esteem, poverty mentality, prejudice, pride, rebellion, self-sabotage, shame, stubbornness, and worry. Contrary to the way it may look, this list is not exhaustive!

What we can do about iniquity is to simply understand that Jesus is the yoke destroyer and we can, by faith, receive the severing of those generations of iniquity in our lives. My analogy is this: If you are a truck, iniquity is a trailer, and sins are boxes on the trailer, we can ask for forgiveness of our sins and they are forgiven, pushed off of the trailer. But we still have the trailer attached to us. Anyone who has ever pulled a trailer knows that you're always looking back. The trailer can sway your vehicle and cause damage or a wreck. Right?

Iniquity is the same. If iniquity is "attached" to us, sins have a place to land. So let's get rid of the trailer of iniquity! Simply take by faith the yoke destroying power of God's love through Jesus, unhitching you from the yoke of iniquity, ask for forgiveness for all the generations behind you and pray a blessing over all the generations ahead you.

Next, trust God. When I prayed this prayer to cut off all iniquity from my life, I saw major changes occur. Thoughts of entitlement turned to humble gratitude. Thoughts of loneliness turned to peace and trust. Thoughts of being disqualified because of my mistakes turned to seeing myself as Christ sees me: out of the ashes, resurrected, made whole, clean, worthy because He says I am. It took time for the tares that were entangled in my life to be bound up and removed but, one day at a time, Holy Spirit and I cleaned up my thoughts so that my actions would line up with Him. God says that I am made in His image. I am His "mini-me." He reached inside of Himself and pulled out a fist-full of His likeness, put some skin on it, and called it Tina LaRea. That's how I see it anyway. I am His and He is mine, and abiding in Him is the way that I believe we can win at dealing with life's challenges.

One of the biggest struggles people have is feeling like they are a failure or dealing with failure in general. What are your views on the topic of dealing with failure?

I remember a time in my life when I was feeling low; actually, very low, the failure of all failures (I thought). I was at rock bottom and I did the only thing I knew to do: seek God with all that was within me. A local church was hosting a Christian band that would be in concert on a weekend that I could go, so I got tickets and went. My seat was way up in the balcony, just a few rows from being the furthest up in the building. As we all sang and worshipped, the building was filled with the electrifying connection of God's love in and for us all. Not a single soul was seated as we all stood the entire concert, hands and voices raised in adoration of our God. It was beautiful. The lead singer of the band began to pray aloud, inquiring of God, "Open up the heavens and let Your glory fall down on us, LORD!" Suddenly, a young man seated to my left and back a couple of rows yelled out, "Send it on me, LORD! Send it on me!" So, I shouted out, "While you're in the neighborhood, send it on me too!" We wrapped up that concert having met the indescribable Elohim and His magnificence in a way that we'd never known, and then I drove to my parents' house where I was staying for the weekend.

The next day, as I walked through my parents' home and headed toward the laundry room, something completely out of this world happened to me. As my feet crossed the threshold of the living room and dining room, God's glorified presence fell on me. In that moment, I could not move forward or backward. I couldn't inhale or exhale. I couldn't raise myself up or fall down. My spirit within me was shouting, "More of you, LORD! More of you!" While my flesh was crying out with a whispered quiver, "I can't take it!" My body felt the resonating flow of electricity running up and down every cell of my body. My skin felt as though billions of tiny air pressure jets were blowing into my skin. I needed to fall. His presence was too great. I had no control. In that moment, I remembered the song, "I Can Only Imagine," and, as I thought through the verses, I realized that I knew the answer to the questions in that song. What will I do when I am in His presence? I will do what He allows. I will not fall unless He allows. I will not raise up unless He allows. I will not advance forward or take a step back unless He allows. Will I speak or be silent? Whatever He allows. Whatever is perfect in Him is what I will do. In His presence, there is nothing averse to Him; He is, and that is all that matters.

What advice would you give to someone who is ready to reclaim and live their sparkle?

I spent thirty years of my adult life just trying to get by, working at jobs that paid the bills but offered no real personal satisfaction. I didn't know my own identity or what my purpose was here in the earth. As an encourager, I helped others succeed in meeting their goals, but I had no idea what my true sparkle even was! I knew some of my talents, but what was my sparkle? My purpose? My passion? The shift came for me in an unexpected invitation.

One day, I sat at a restaurant table visiting with my friend Elli, when she looked at me and said, "Tina, I think you should consider taking the Art Mastery Program at the Milan Art Institute. I have only two spots available, and I'd like for you to take one." I replied, "Why would I do that? I'm not an artist. I can barely paint my face! Besides, I've been accepted into one of America's most elite entrepreneurial programs and I'm scheduled to begin in September." She said, "I just think you should consider it. Please pray about it."

So, I prayed, and I thought about it this way: if I had only one year of my life left to live, where would I really want to invest my time? I decided that I really wanted to spend the next year with my friend Elli, to be in her presence and in the presence of her family. If I never sold a single piece of art, I would never regret having spent time with these precious souls. If I wanted to, I could re-apply to the entrepreneurial program the next year. So, with absolutely NO background in art and completely stepping out on faith, I made the call and told Elli that I would take the Art Mastery Program. This is where my sparkle really began to shine, my unique voice began taking shape, and the layers of my personality and giftings began unfolding. For the first time in my life, at the age of 50, I was in my lane, doing what I was created to do, living my sparkle! I would say to trust the leading of the Holy Spirit, go in the way of peace, and sparkle on!

What "must have" resources would you recommend someone use daily in keeping focused, motivated, and encouraged?

Number one priority resource: a personal, intimate relationship and walk with the Triune God. He is your greatest "must have" resource for all things!

Next, I'd say your own mouth. Speak LIFE into your situation. Be sure that your mouth is speaking what you want to manifest in your life and in the lives of your loved ones. When I speak, I want my words to be something that the Triune God can come into agreement with; that way, I have three witnesses to establish what I'm speaking. Jesus is High Priest over my confession. By the witness of just two, a thing is established in the earth. Therefore, I purpose to speak life-giving, positive words and not to speak accusatory words or doubt or death.

For spiritual items, I recommend a Bible and a prayer journal (at the very least). In my prayer journal, I like to list the topic or person that I am praying about, put the date, and write in red ink the Scripture upon which I am basing my faith for that prayer. I speak LIFE into that topic or person and wait to see the manifestation of my prayer. When the prayer is answered, I cross out the prayer and write the date the answer manifested. This is one practical method that has worked very well for me.

For goals that I want to achieve in life, I use resources from Terri Savelle Foy and a calendar, and I would recommend these to others as well. Terri's Dream Big set helps me to write my visions for each thing that I want in my life. I have listed places where I want to travel, restaurants that I want to try, how much weight I want to lose, and items that I want to purchase. As each goal is attained, I cross it off the list and put the date of achievement next to it. You can find Terri's resources on her website at www.terri.com.

Through a personal relationship with God, speaking life, prayer, journaling, reading your Bible, writing your vision and accomplishing your goals, are a few ways I would recommend keeping focused, motivated, and encouraged. But even in all of that, I'd add this: give yourself lots of grace in your pursuit of excellence. Your past doesn't define you. Your broken road is your preparation, your launching pad to your purpose.

Please share 5 of your favorite scriptures, quotes or poems that you have referenced when you needed encouragement.

"I can do all things through Christ who strengthens me." Philippians 4:13

"Death and life are in the power of the tongue, and those who love it will eat its fruit." Proverbs 18:21

"And whether you turn to the right or turn to the left, your ears will hear a message behind you: 'This is the way, walk in it.'" Isaiah 30:21

"If you have built castles in the air, your work need not be lost; that is where they should be. Now put the foundations under them." Henry David Thoreau

"Do the best you can until you know better. Then when you know better, do better." Maya Angelou

What makes you a woman that is an overcomer?

On a Tuesday night in 2004, my daughter and I were watching the 38th Annual Country Music Awards. Not far into the show, I suddenly felt an excruciating pain in my abdomen. The pain gripped me so badly that the painfully screaming voice coming out of my mouth didn't even sound like me! My daughter, nine years old at the time, laid hands on me and prayed and then ran to the neighbors' house to get help. By the time they arrived, the pain had subsided, so I sent them back home and just rested.

The next morning, I sought immediate medical attention and was assigned to a doctor in Huntsville, Texas. He and his nurse examined me TWICE and, onto the back of his notepad, he sketched a picture of what he felt. He said, "You have a cyst hanging on the left side of your uterus. It is in the shape of a 'y' and in the consistency of cauliflower. My nurse is going to schedule you for special imaging at the imaging center here locally and then we'll need to immediately remove the cyst in surgery." The nurse scheduled my imaging for the early the next morning. Surgery would be Friday.

On that Wednesday night, I went to church and, when the altar call was opened for people to pray, I went forward and prayed with a young couple. I told them my story about the cyst and then we prayed and I took, by faith, my healing. But then the young man said something very important to me. He said, "Tina, we've all prayed and come into agreement with God's word and you have received your healing; but now it's your job to keep it!" I'd never heard that before. He went on to say, "The way you keep your healing is you let no words come out of your mouth that are opposite of what God says, regardless of any report you may see or hear. You speak by faith what is done." I said I would and thanked them both for believing with me.

The next morning, I went into the imaging center and had 75 pictures made of my abdomen, 25 of those were taken internally. The doctors and nurses were very quiet, looking my pictures over and over, holding them up under the light, walking out to discuss some things, coming back in and looking again. After some time of this, I asked what was going on. They said, "We can't find a thing wrong! That tumor is GONE!" Hallelujah!

I know that my daughter's faith, the young couple's faith at church, and my faith came together and overcame a physical challenge in my body. Anytime a person gains victory in an area, they have overcome that obstacle and are, therefore, an overcomer. I am blessed in my overcoming so that I can be a blessing to others in helping them overcome. "For whatsoever is born of God overcomes the world: and this is the victory that overcomes the world, even our faith." 1 John 5:4

TINA LAREA

 Tina LaRea is a mixed media artist born and raised in Texas and trained in Arizona. Her creative interests explore the poetics of authenticity, excellence, and love. Through the exploration of diverse materials and techniques, ranging from drawing to installation, she probes into the representations of life, love and freedom, bringing to attention the fragility and strength of brokenness and restoration, being true to oneself while helping others along their journey, that each person has a story that deserves to be told.

Tina LaRea resides in Arizona where she works as an artist and is trained at the Milan Art Institute.

Phone: 480-331-7014
Address: 4848 E. Cactus Rd. Ste. 505-225, Scottsdale, AZ 85254
Email: tinalarea@tinalarea.com
Email: tinalarea@gmail.com
Website: www.tinalarea.com / www.tinalarea.art

LISA CORRALES

What one word would you use to describe yourself and why did you choose that word?

Determined. I chose determined because I truly want to fulfill God's purpose for my life.

Share with us about an experience you faced that challenged you and placed you in a situation where you had to make tough decisions?

After being a wife, mother of 5 and completely immersing myself in that role for most of my adult life; I found myself at the age of 43 divorced and living in a bedroom in my parents' home. I had to determine how to reinvent myself, provide for myself and my teenage daughter. And most of all I had to hear from God and understand what the next step was. What He had in store for me and how He might lead me there.

How did you overcome it?

First and foremost, I found myself asking God for grace, mercy, and forgiveness so I could begin to heal, move past the veil of guilt and begin to clearly see what the next step was.

In His faithfulness, He began to shed just enough light for me to see the beginnings of my new journey. As I learned to trust Him with each new step, He began to reveal His plans for my life which were greater than anything I could have dreamed for myself. I had no idea what I was even good at other than raising children! I came to a point where I just said, "Father I want your dreams for me not mine That's when He slowly, day by day started guiding me to what He had for me.

I would literally get up every morning and just say, "Ok daddy put the right people in my path today and lead me as to what you want me to do." He would!!! Every day was a step-in learning to trust Him with my future and my life. The job I thought I had to have so my children could be in the school they needed to be in would just not come together, as hard as I knocked on the doors and called every week I kept hitting a brick wall. Thank you Father for protecting me! He had so much more for me than I could fathom for myself!

While waiting on that job to happen I started a cleaning business. I could be in and out of a house in a few hours, make good money, save to buy pieces of furniture or anything else that I could put a coat of paint on!! I would clean in the morning and paint furniture until midnight, get up and do it all again the next day for a year and a half.

One day I stopped by this old rundown building in town to pick up a piece of junk that smelled SO BAD I had to drive home with the windows rolled down! EVERY piece I bought there stunk to high heaven! That day the guy who was renting the building said, "You should buy this place Lisa", I thought, you have lost your mind buddy! Why would I want this? As soon as I had that thought I remembered a dream I had a few weeks earlier about that old building, down to the color of the walls and ivy growing up the sides. Hmmm? I think God wants me to buy this old building. I had 15 thousand dollars in cash to my name and was saving it for a little house in town that the folks who owned it had told me I could buy when they got through all the legal mess they were going through. The father had passed away and they were having to deal with everything that goes along with that. We met with the man who owned the old dilapidated building and asked him what he wanted for it. He gave us a price, my dad countered, I just stood there like a knot on a log. Remember, I knew nothing about nothing except raising children! The sweet man said," I need 30 thousand down". My dad said," She will give you 15 thousand now and 15 thousand in 6 months". Holy smoke daddy! Are you kidding! Oh well, there went my 15 thousand for my house and Lord only knows where the rest was going to come from in 6 months!

So, it took a month for the building to get cleaned out! It was disgusting to say the least. I bought it, walked in, and sat on the old concrete floor and cried! What have I done Lord? I now have a run-down building that I have no idea what to do with and NO money! I had no idea why He wanted me to buy it in the first place! Again, I was learning to trust Him with everything. On a warm Sunday afternoon, a few weeks later I walked in the old building, not in a good mood, honestly just flat out mad. I took a sledge hammer to every wall I could hit! I was working out a little bit of oh poor me! boo hoo.

In that process I started thinking, "Hmmm, I could put my workshop in this back room and give my precious parents back their garage that I had turned into a Sanford and Son set". God bless my parents, they were so sweet and encouraging, I'm sure they thought they were never going to get rid of me! I mean I was 43 at this point and had taken over their garage for over a year. However, they encouraged me my whole life. A parents' work is never done.

So, I moved all my junk, I mean treasures, into the back room of my old building. I would clean houses during the day and paint furniture till the wee hours, and I loved every minute of it. Boy how my life had changed. I had gone from living in a mansion in Dallas to a bedroom in my parents' home and cleaning houses. However, I was determined to not live on alimony, I knew God had something more for me and I was ready to find out! I was just so happy to be stepping into whatever it was.

Well low and behold the 6 months came fast! It was time for that balloon payment and I had NO idea where that 15 thousand was coming from. I just said, "Father you told me to buy this thing so I'm depending on you to supply me with the money". Well guess what? Two weeks before I had to make that payment I got a check in the mail, my step grandfather had passed away months earlier and had left me a gift. It was enough to make that payment with 14 thousand left over!

My dad had people looking at the building to get estimates, and they would all say, "Umm it will take at least 50 to 75 thousand to redo this and honestly we don't know if we want to touch it". We knew God came to my rescue, He spoke to my heart, "Give me that 14 thousand and let me show you what we can do with it." So, I found a man that agreed to fix the roof and I lined up everyone else behind him. He showed up on a Monday morning, walked around it and said, don't think I want to do this lady". At this point my faith was growing so much that I didn't even blink. I knew God had this and would bring me someone else to do the job.

I called an old friend of my dad's, asked him if he knew anyone who could help me and sure enough he did! God brought me the sweetest angel of a man named brother Jimmy. He agreed to stay three weeks, fix my roof and do all my drywall inside. That precious angel of a man looked at me one day and said, "Sister, I'm supposed to stay here and help you as long as you need me". He ended up staying 3 months. I know to this day God put that sweet man in my life to keep me inspired and encouraged every day. Lord knows he had his work cut out for him. I was mouthy and a mess. I'm sure he took on way more than he had anticipated. But he just kept encouraging me the whole way through. To this day, I don't think there is anything I would not do for that dear man.

Three months later I opened my little shop and called it THE RED DOOR. I had a hand full of merchandise to sell but I didn't see it that way. I was just so excited! Well God blessed it, and I worked hard every day. It has grown every year. He got me through some tough years during the recession but I have never been in the red. We like to call Him Jehovah, nick of time around our house! He never failed me. Sometimes I didn't know where the money was going to come from to pay those bills but He always came through. He had His work cut out for Him though, I think our memory is so short sometimes! It took years for me to realize as long as He wanted me there He would pay the bills. I needed keep doing what He puts before me and He would take care of me.

In case you are wondering about the house I had been waiting on, God gave me that too. We will save that testimony for another day! I just can't tell you how good He is to his children and how much He wants us to just ask Him for help! Every day that walk out of my shop I turn around, look at it in disbelief that He gave me something so much more than I could have ever dreamed for! I had no idea what I even wanted. However, HE did!

I have had my shop for 12 years now and have looked forward to going to work every day to just see what He has in store for me that day. It has been such an amazing chapter of my life, getting to love on people every day. I get up every morning and say, "Ok father, I'm ready to get to work. Use me today, let me be your hands, your feet, your voice". One thing I have learned is God doesn't ask for perfection, He ask for availability. I'm just so thankful He lets me be a part of His work. Sometimes life just doesn't turn out the way that we have it planned. Thank you Father for giving us more than one chance at this thing and showing us our gifts, talents and abilities that you instilled in us in the womb to fulfill your purpose for our life!!!

Staying motivated when things don't seem to be coming together is a challenge at times. How do you motivate yourself?

Initially I had to overcome doubt and fear so I immediately go back to the scripture God gave me in the beginning of my journey, Jeremiah 29;11, "For I know the plans I have for you declares the Lord, plans to prosper you not to harm you, plans to give you a hope and a future".

What would you advise someone else?

To get truly honest with themselves, then get honest with God about yourself, to the point of being naked and completely vulnerable, while placing your life in His Hands. He will never lead you to something without equipping you to do it.

In your opinion, what does it really take to win at dealing with life challenges?

Stay focused, be in constant prayer, know He's got your back! Don't try to look too far down the road. Lord knows today is enough to deal with, just trust Him with the step you are on, knowing He will give you just enough light to take the next step. Keep that childlike faith and for goodness sakes, try to keep a sense of humor. He's got you girl!

One of the biggest struggles people have is feeling like they are a failure or dealing with failure in general. What are your views on the topic of dealing with failure?

Everyone at some point in their life is going to face failure of some kind. If this life was all kittens and puppies, we wouldn't need HIM! For some it's as simple as not completing a task, for others, it may be dealing with a weight issue. For me, personally it was the failure of my 25-year marriage. One of the side effects of failure is the horrible overwhelming guilt that inevitably consumes you. For me, the first step in dealing with it was realizing for the first time in my life that my heavenly father was not holding a big cosmic stick ready to strike me down.

Instead He was ready and willing to pick me up right where I was, show me His amazing love, mercy and grace that had been there all along. I had the strength to begin healing so, I could move forward and grasp the incredible future he had for me. one that was so much more than I could ever fathom for myself. it was a grieving process much like one experiences with a death of a close friend.

I'm not saying it was easy in fact it was the most painful part of this journey, the place where I began to overcome all my doubt and fear and make the shift to begin seeing the failure as an opportunity to learn, trust, and grow.

What advice would you give to someone who is ready to reclaim and live their sparkle?

To meet each day with excitement, gratitude and a new-found confidence to accomplish everything He puts before you.

What "must have" resources would you recommend someone use daily in keeping focused, motivated, and encouraged?

A consistent routine of daily devotionals. My personal favorite is Jesus Calling by Sarah Young, uplifting scriptures, and most important prayer. I have found that the practice of encouraging others allows me to also be encouraged, keeps me grounded in gratitude, and focused on my true purpose in life.

Please share 5 of your favorites scriptures, quotes or poems that you have referenced when you needed encouragement.

As I mentioned earlier Jeremiah 29;11 has been the scripture that has helped me through some of the most challenging times of my life. "For I know the plans I have for you says the Lord. They are plans for good and not for evil, to give you a future and a hope".

Another favorite is, Psalms 91, "Whoever dwells in the shelter of the Most High will rest in the shadow of the Almighty. 2 I will say of the LORD, "He is my refuge and my fortress, my God, in whom I trust." 3 Surely he will save you from the fowler's snare and from the deadly pestilence. 4 He will cover you with his feathers, and under his wings you will find refuge; his faithfulness will be your shield and rampart. 5 You will not fear the terror of night, nor the arrow that flies by day, 6 nor the pestilence that stalks in the darkness, nor the plague that destroys at midday. 7 A thousand may fall at your side, ten thousand at your right hand, but it will not come near you. 8 You will only observe with your eyes and see the punishment of the wicked. 9 If you say, "The LORD is my refuge," and you make the Most High your dwelling, 10 no harm will overtake you, no disaster will come near your tent. 11 For he will command his angels concerning you to guard you in all your ways; 12 they will lift you up in their hands, so that you will not strike your foot against a stone. 13 You will tread on the lion and the cobra; you will trample the great lion and the serpent. 14 "Because he loves me," says the LORD, "I will rescue him; I will protect him, for he acknowledges my name. 15 He will call on me, and I will answer him; I will be with him in trouble, I will deliver him and honor him. 16 With long life I will satisfy him and show him my salvation."

Philippians 4:6-8 "Don't worry about anything; instead; pray about everything; tell God your needs and don't forget to thank Him for his answers. If you do this you will experience God's peace, which is far more wonderful than the human mind can understand. His peace will keep your thoughts and your hearts quiet at rest as you trust in Jesus Christ. And now, brothers, as I close this letter let me say this one more thing; Fix your thoughts on what is true and good and right. Think about things that are pure and lovely, and dwell on the fine, good things in others. think about all you can praise God for and be glad about."

Romans 12:12 "Be glad for all God is planning for you. be patient in trouble, and prayerful always."

Romans 8:28 "And we know that all that happens to us is working for our good if we love God and are fitting in His plans."

Philippians 4:13 "For I can do everything God asks me to with the help of Jesus Christ who gives me the strength and power."

What makes you a woman that is an overcomer?

I would have to go back to the one word I used to describe myself; determined. I am determined to experience everything God has for me in this life! It's like a book, there are many chapters, don't get stuck on one and not experience them all, learn what He is trying to teach you in each chapter so you can move on to the next!! This life is a vapor, now that I have 8 grand babies I can tell you, it flies by!! Enjoy and make the most of EVERYTHING and every challenge he puts before you. if He did it for a little girl from wildwood, Florida who thought her life was over, He can do it for you! again, He isn't up there with a huge cosmic stick wanting to knock us down when we mess up. Quite the opposite my friend, He wants to pick you up put His loving arms around us wipe the dirt and tears away and get us back on track! he just loves us so much. Now get on with it girlfriend!! Go live your sparkle!!!!

LISA CORRALES

I was born November 2, 1960 in Ocala, Florida. I grew up with 2 brothers and wonderful parents who owned a shoe and clothing store in Wildwood, Florida. I was taught an amazing work ethic from 7 yrs. old running the register on a stool and fitting people for shoes!

My whole childhood I just dreamed of the life I would have one day as a mother and wife. So, at the age of 18 I got married and 16 months later had the first of 5 children in 10 years! Lacy, Lindsey, Laney, Whitt, and Lexi and we lived in Texas, Tennessee and back to Dallas in the 90s where I met Yvonne George! Although I immersed myself in my family my marriage of 25 yrs. fell apart soon after we moved back to Florida in 2003. I had to learn how to re-invent myself quickly. I was beyond blessed to have met a wonderful man frank, who I have been married to for 11 years.

I have owned a home and garden store THE RED DOOR for 12 years where God has shown me I have more gifts, talents and abilities than I ever thought! it has been a wonderful ministry where I get to love on people every day! Last year I was presented the business woman of the year award! me?? Really!!

I've truly loved this chapter of my life but a few months ago I felt God leading me into a new chapter. It's scary to say the least, I have poured my heart and soul into my shop for so long and never dreamed of doing anything else but it's time to start enjoying all my blessings and that includes 8 grand babies!! Plus, we have been part of planting a new church here and feel like God is calling me into different areas of ministry. I can't help but get excited about this next chapter, I'm not sure what it all entails, but if there is one thing I have learned through this journey its He wants to use us until the day we kick! That's the only way we will ever be truly happy and fulfilled! I know this next chapter will be exciting, I can't wait to get started!! Who knows where and what He will take me into but I will be ready to sparkle whatever it may be!!!

Email: lisathereddoor@yahoo.com
Facebook: www.facebook.com/lisa.h.corrales
Phone: 352-216-1206

PRESENTED BY:
YVONNE GEORGE

Yvonne was born and raised in Longview Texas. Raised as a small-town girl with big city dreams. Yvonne always had plans for a bright future and could not wait to move to the big city. However, at the age of 12, Yvonne unexpectedly lost her father to an aneurysm and her dreams seemed shattered. She was forced to dig deep as a child as she mourned the loss of her dad, and yet try to provide comfort to her mother at the same time. This huge life event prompted Yvonne to never take life for granted and realize each day was a gift.

Yvonne George has been in the in the fashion industry for more than 25 years. She became known as a fashion expert and her reputation grew, becoming a shining star, known as the "Sparkle Guru." Appearing as a guest on the Penny Gilley Show on RFD-TV, as well as serving as Penny's stylist! (RFD-TV is a cable and satellite network channel devoted to Rural America and is seen in 47.3 million homes.)

Yvonne is also CEO/Founder of own Lifestyle brand called Live your Sparkle which was created especially for women to transform their lives from ordinary to extraordinary through the power of Sparkle. This endeavor is a strategic approach to empower, inspire and motivate women through the power of sparkle.

Made in the USA
San Bernardino, CA
04 June 2017